2-24-60

SIXTH ANNUAL WINDSOR LECTURES *THE FAMILY SAGA*

University of Illinois Press, Urbana, 1958

THE
FAMILY
SAGA

AND OTHER PHASES OF AMERICAN FOLKLORE

MODY C. BOATRIGHT

ROBERT B. DOWNS

JOHN T. FLANAGAN

© 1958 by The Board of Trustees of the University of Illinois
Manufactured in the United States of America

FOREWORD

The lectures which follow constitute the sixth series of the Phineas L. Windsor Lectures in Librarianship. The Windsor Lectures were endowed by the Alumni Association of the University of Illinois Library School in 1948. The money for the fund was contributed by graduates of the School to honor Mr. Windsor upon his retirement in 1940 following thirty-one years of exceptional service to the University as director of the Library School and the Library.

The five previous series have been published, quite handsomely indeed, by the University of Illinois Press. One, *Bibliography in an Age of Science,* by Louis Ridenour, Ralph Shaw, and Albert G. Hill, was chosen by the American Institute of Graphic Arts as one of the fifty best books of that year. It has also made a considerable mark for itself in the scholarly world, if frequent quotation in other published works may be considered a gauge. Another, *Three Presidents and Their Books,* by Arthur Bestor, David Mearns, and Jonathan Daniels, has been singled out for special attention in the current catalog of Sears, Roebuck and Company as one of twelve outstanding books on American culture, an unexpected but not unappreciated recognition.

Between these two and the remaining volumes, *Three Lantern Slides,* by John T. Winterich, *Nineteenth Century English Books,* by Gordon Ray, Carl Weber, and John Carter, and *Books and the Mass Market,* by Harold Guinzburg, Robert Frase, and Theodore Waller, it is possible to find a slender linking thread. All of the lectures recorded therein are concerned, however diversely, with some aspect or problem of book publishing, book production, book distribution, book use, or book reading.

To embrace, comfortably, such a widely variegated range of subjects requires a definition of "librarianship" of some elasticity. Now it must, as some have already observed, be stretched a bit more to cover this new series. To base our definition upon the common quality of a "concern with books" is a possibility, despite the fact that the folk tale, as Archer Taylor describes it, is "a narrative of anonymous origin, in *oral* circulation." However, I am told on reliable authority that capture and imprisonment in print does not destroy the organic quality of the folk tale so long as it does not remove it from word-of-mouth communication by the common folk. The folklorist, who is, apparently, from but not of the masses, in recording a tale makes it available for study and for comparison by other folklorists. Their books are then, quite obviously, worthwhile additions to libraries, and thus a part of librarianship.

That folk tales are of interest — consuming interest — needs no remarking. Ancient in origin, constantly rejuvenated in their retelling, they have the vitality of eternal youth. And the hearers are legion, an audience itself continuously renewed.

The three authors for this series on "The Family Saga and Other Phases of American Folklore" are undoubtedly experts in this subject. They have heard the tales, have recorded them against loss, have reflected upon their characteristics and qualities. Better than being mere experts they are appreciators, and the reader is bound to be the happier for it.

In this day of science let us rejoice that there is nothing scientific in what they tell us. Instead of dissection with the sharp scapel to lay bare sanguinary and unappealing details of insides, they hold their objects to the light so that we may catch their brilliance and their color.

In an interesting way, the Messrs. Boatright, Downs, and Flanagan represent the three known species of the genus folklorist. There are some who find the lore, and record it. These are the field men and Mr. Boatright is of this group. There are others who interpret the lore, seeking its meanings, observing the variants, clarifying the allusions. These are exemplified by Mr. Downs. Finally, there are those who read the tales with the critic's sharp eye, evaluating their place in, and contribution to, the larger national literature. Of these Mr. Flanagan is an outstanding example.

To set the scene let me merely say that there are many kinds of folk tales. Among the better known is the *myth* which generally tells of the gods, the *fairy story* of impossible fantasy, the *etiological tale* which explains the origins of things, the *historical tale* which sounds authentic but is often apocryphal, the *jest,* the *tall tale* of outrageous exaggeration, and the *fable* with its practical wisdom or moral overtones.

They are found, in all their forms, all over the world, and folk tales have been the instruments of amusement, and education, since time immemorial. The subject is extensive and ramified. In this brief book comprehensive consideration is impossible. Thus the authors have limited themselves not only to American folklore, but to three particular aspects or facets of it.

Professor Mody C. Boatright, who contributes the first lecture, was born deep in the land where tall tales grow. It's grand country as we all know. Pitchfork Tillman used to say, "Texas has more trees and less timber, more rivers and less water, more resources and less cash, more preachers and less religion, more cows and less milk, and you can see farther and see less than in any damn country in the world." Naturally no man in his right mind would ever leave so wondrous a place, and Mody Boatright never did. He was born in Texas, educated in Texas, and has taught in Texas, for a short while at Sul Ross State Teachers College, but since 1926 at the University at Austin. He has been a mainstay of the Texas Folklore Society for many years, editing many of its publications. *Folk Laughter on the American Frontier* (from which came Pitchfork Tillman's description), *Tall Tales from Texas,* and *Gib Morgan, Minstrel of the Oil Fields,* are the satisfying titles of his major books. On him has been placed the mantle of one of the greatest of all students of Western lore, his teacher, friend, and colleague, James Frank Dobie.

Mr. Robert B. Downs, Dean of Library Administration and Director of the University of Illinois Library School and author of the second lecture, has understood and enjoyed folklore since his early boyhood in North Carolina. He, like Mr. Boatright, came from one of those sections of our country where the folk tale is germinated and nurtured, in this case the old and lovely hills around Asheville. As so many Southerners, Mr. Downs has always been known to his intimates as an infectious storyteller whose particular forte is the desiccated anecdote of wry and unexpected twist. A large audience has known his pamphlet, "American Humorous Folklore."

Professor John T. Flanagan comes from the Paul Bunyan country. Born, raised, and educated in Minnesota, he made one tentative sortie into the Boatright region to the South. During one year at Southern Methodist University in Dallas he became increasingly doubtful of Texan veracity and decided to return to the land of honest men. He has been an ornament of the University of Illinois, seeking after the truth, since 1946.

He is an acknowledged student of regional literature. Max Lerner only the other day called Mr. Flanagan's *America Is West* the best of the Midwest anthologies. Very shortly another book from Mr. Flanagan's pen, entitled *Folklore in American Literature,* will reach the bookstalls. An earlier volume was *James Hall, Literary Pioneer of the Ohio Valley.*

His field of study has fitted him particularly for foreign assignments as a lecturer on American writing and authors. This he has done with notable success in Kyoto, Nice, and Bordeaux, despite the fact that as he does not enjoy wine he was clearly wasted in the latter great center of French viniculture.

Not long ago the University Library acquired the Franklin J. Meine collection of some 8,500 volumes of prose, verse, and cartoons on the funny, ridiculous, and whimsical in American culture. This collection was secured largely through the interest and efforts of Professor Flanagan.

The three speakers provided for their auditors at the University of Illinois Library School during March, 1958, three pleasant, profitable, and wholly adult evenings. Through this book the Library School is happy that these pleasures may be enjoyed by many far beyond the confines of Urbana.

HAROLD LANCOUR
Associate Director
University of Illinois
Library School

CONTENTS

The Family Saga as a Form of Folklore   *1*

MODY C. BOATRIGHT

Apocryphal Biology: A Chapter in American Folklore   *20*

ROBERT B. DOWNS

Folklore in American Literature   *49*

JOHN T. FLANAGAN

MODY C. BOATRIGHT

THE FAMILY SAGA AS A FORM OF FOLKLORE

It is with some hesitancy that I apply the term "family saga" to the subject of this paper. I am not here concerned with the heroic poems of Ireland or Iceland or the North European continent, dealing with battles and trials of strength and the complex genealogies of heroes. Nor may the narratives with which I am concerned be accurately called American analogues to these European works. I use the term mainly to denote a lore that tends to cluster around families, or often the patriarchs or matriarchs of families, which is preserved and modified by oral transmission, and which is believed to be true. Lore that is handed down *as* folklore is excluded. I am, then, not concerned with a type of tale, but with clusters of types, not with a motif, but with many motifs.

These clusters never form a connected history. Such a coherent narrative requires research in libraries and archives.[1] A history or biography written wholly or largely from oral sources has its values, but they are not the values of history or biography.

---

[1] From the number of genealogists who clutter up the Barker Texas History Center, where I sometimes work, I estimate that a million people are at work on such histories.

1

What Homer Croy learned from the neighbors of Jesse James was folklore, a part of the James family saga.[2]

A consideration of these clusters of lore raises a number of questions, for which I have no final answers: What forms and motifs make up the family saga? What is their relation to history? What kinds of historical incidents survive in the oral tradition with little change? How do incidents, some historical and some folk tales of great antiquity, become incorporated into the family saga?

First, the general observation may be made that each episode has, in Martha Beckwith's phrase, "taken on, through . . . repetition and variation, the character of a group composition," and that it "functions in the emotional life of the folk."[3] For a tale to enter the oral tradition and survive, it must afford emotional satisfaction to the hearers, who then repeat the tale and thus widen and continue its circulation. Nothing could be duller and, even when a product of the imagination, further removed from folklore than inventories of property and lists of offices of honor and trust held by one's ancestors.

An event in the family saga has a relation to a social context and reflects a social value. This does not mean, however, that the event is invariably in harmony with the actual social conditions of the region where it is believed to have happened. Two examples will illustrate this lack of harmony.

In one Texas family it is believed that an ancestress, during the Civil War, seeing a group of Union soldiers approaching the farm, began hiding the things of most value. Her most valued possession was a jewel box and its contents of diamonds, rubies, emeralds, and pearls. It developed that her fears were unfounded, for the soldiers were looking only for food, and when they had obtained it they left, and the mother and children began restoring the hidden articles to their proper places. But

---

[2] Homer Croy, *Jesse James Was My Neighbor* (New York, 1947).

[3] Martha Warren Beckwith, *Folklore in America,* Publications of the Folklore Foundation, No. 11 (Poughkeepsie, 1930), p. 3.

for some reason the jewel box was left in hiding. A few days later the mother died very suddenly, and the box, in spite of long and repeated searches, has never been found.

Now since Texas, where the family lived, was never invaded by Union soldiers, either the time or place is wrong. It could be that the troops were those of the occupation after the war; it could be that the story was transferred from the deep South, where the accepted thing was for the mistress of the plantation to bury the silver and jewels or have them carried off by the Yankees. If you wish, you may say that here is an etiological tale explaining the absence of family jewels.

In Massachusetts the accepted thing is for your ancestors to have been abolitionists associated with the underground railroad. Nathaniel Benchley, in a biography of Robert Benchley, writes of the first Benchley "to attract attention in Worchester" that after a political career, first as state senator and then as Lieutenant Governor, he, "feeling that the slavery problem needed more attention than he could give it from the Statehouse . . . went to Texas and set up a station on the underground railroad, helping slaves escape to the North. He was caught, convicted, and spent the rest of the time until Appomattox in a Texas jail."[4]

All this seemed rather strange to a certain Texas historian, Andrew Forest Muir. In the first place there was no reason for helping Texas slaves escape to the North, when Mexico, which welcomed Negroes and granted them full equality, was many times nearer than Canada. Muir looked into the records and established that Henry W. Benchley was in Texas as early as April 12, 1859; that he taught singing lessons first in San Antonio and then in Houston; that after the Confederate Congress had passed an act exempting railroad employees from military service, he was a conductor on the Houston and Texas Central Railroad; and that on one occasion he got up a musical entertainment for Confederate troops. He never went to jail in

---

[4] Nathaniel Benchley, *Robert Benchley, A Biography* (New York, 1955), p. 21.

Texas, and the railroad with which he was connected ran upon a flat coastal plain where not even a single tunnel was required.[5]

The tale clearly originated in Massachusetts in conformity with a pattern of conduct people of that state expect of their ancestors. It does not conform to a long tradition about why people came to Texas.

Long before Texas was a subject of concern to the people of the United States, it was assumed by the conservative well-to-do that anybody who left for the frontier did so for a good but hardly laudable reason.[6] Timothy Dwight thought that the people leaving New England must be a sorry lot, and Virginians used to say of one who left that state that he had gone to Hell or Kentucky. When people from the United States began moving into Texas and the political implications of foreseen annexation became apparent, the tradition that the frontiersman was a fugitive became intensified and localized. Thus a sort of archetype was created, which the Texans did little to refute. Samuel Adams Hammett, who was in Texas from 1835 to 1847, after writing a defense of the settlers, remarked that they were partly to blame for "the contumely heaped upon them. [They] indulged in a sly chuckle over their somewhat dubious reputation, and it was a common joke to ask a man what his name at home was and what he came to Texas for."[7] And according to W. B. Dewees, an early Texas settler, the answer would be, "for some crime or other which they had committed . . . if they deny having committed any crime, and say they did not run away, they are generally looked upon rather suspiciously. Those who come into the country at the present time [1831] frequently tell us rough, ragged, old settlers . . . that they have a great deal of wealth

---

[5] Andrew Forest Muir, "The Skelton in Robert Benchley's Closet," *The Southwest Review,* XLIII (Winter, 1958), 70-72. To point out the inaccuracy of the story is not to convict Nathaniel Benchley of anything more serious than failure to verify what he set down as fact.

[6] Mody C. Boatright, *Folk Laughter on the American Frontier* (New York, 1949), pp. 1-15.

[7] Samuel Adams Hammett, *A Stray Yankee in Texas* (second edition, New York, 1858), p. 4.

in the States, which they are going after as soon as they find a situation to suit them. But we not relishing this would-be aristocracy generally manage to play a good joke on them in return."[8] One day when a number of these would-be aristocrats were boasting of their "lands and Negroes and their ships at sea," they were thus addressed by "Old Man Macfarlane":

"Well, gentlemen," he said, "I too once commenced telling that I had left a large property in the States, and in fact, gentlemen, I told the story so often that at length I really believed it true, and eventually started to go for it. Well, I travelled on very happily till I reached the Sabine River. . . . On its banks I paused, and now for the first time began to ask myself, What am I doing! Why am I here! I have no property in the States, and if I did, if I cross the river 'tis at the risk of my life, for I was obliged to flee to this country to escape punishment of the laws. I had better return and live in safety as I have done. I did so, gentlemen, and since that time have been contented without telling of the wealth I left in the States."[9]

The boasters were so angry that they would have injured the old man had his friends not intervened, but this "put a stop to their long yarns."

This attitude of the early settlers has persisted among their descendants, and many a Texas family saga begins with a G.T.T. — gone to Texas — story. That of Dandy Jim Smith will serve as an example.

In 1846, when Dandy Jim was a youth in Tennessee, there were in the community in which he lived two factions: the Mountain Boys and the Valley Boys, or the hill boys and the plantation boys. They crashed each other's parties and dances and had numerous fist fights. Then the Valley Boys brought knives into action, and the arms race was on. The Mountain Boys went to a Valley Boys' dance on a river boat with hickory clubs concealed in their pantlegs. The fight began on signal. A

---

[8] W. B. Dewees, *Letters from an Early Texas Settler*, compiled by Clara Corlelle (second edition, Louisville, 1853), p. 135.
[9] *Ibid.*

Valley Boy drew a pistol and shot a Mountain Boy in the knee. But the clubs were more effective than the single pistol, and many a Valley Boy was knocked off into the river. Some climbed back in their wet clothes and re-entered the fight, but when it was over, thirteen were missing. A mob formed and began rounding up the Mountain Boys. But not Jim and his brother Watt. They hid in a cave, where an old fisherwoman brought them food. They eventually got to Texas after shooting two of their pursuers.

I do not know that "Old Man Macfarlane" ever committed a crime in his life, nor do I know why Dandy Jim Smith came to Texas. I have told the story as I have had it from his descendants,[10] and I shall not offend them by trying to refute it.

Its significance in this context does not depend upon its accuracy as a biographical event. It is one example of the continuation of a long tradition with many variants. Sometimes it is the over-successful duelist who flees. Sometimes two men fight on a bridge; one is knocked into the river and drowns, the other goes to Texas. But the deed, whatever it is, must not indicate a criminal mind. It must not be robbery, embezzlement, or murder with malice aforethought. If any of these were the real crime, then the family saga would have to make a substitution or remain silent.

The saga of a pioneer family, as would be expected, will include adventures with wild animals. Because the frontiersman was armed with a superior rifle, and because he had been sufficiently touched by the Enlightenment to look upon the animals as natural creatures that could be killed with powder and lead, these adventures rarely exhibit the superstitious fear characteristic of the older Indo-European folklore. The typical hunt had little in it to catch the popular fancy. As Jim Doggett put it, "It is told in two sentences — a bar is started, and he is killed.

---

[10] Angelina Smith, "Dandy Jim Smith," unpublished manuscript. This is largely a collection of tales gathered by Floyd Smith from "various relatives and old-timers," that is to say, from oral sources.

The thing is somewhat monotonous."[11] Stories that pass into the oral tradition are likely to reveal (1) the uncommon sagacity of the hunter or (2) show human beings in jeopardy.

The first is exemplified by a story of how Adam Lawrence[12] relieved the starving colony. It was a time of prolonged drought and all the game had left the country, though crows occasionally flew over. Lawrence shot one to learn what it had been eating, and found an acorn in its craw. He knew there "was plenty of fat game where that crow drew his rations." He led a party in the direction the crows had come from, and after traveling many miles, they found oak trees and fat buffalo, bear, deer, and elk.[13]

For a story placing a human being in jeopardy, the panther was the favored animal. He, of course, was not a man-hunter, and it was said that a man could take a willow switch and a feist dog and drive him out of the country. But he would fight when cornered, he might be attracted by the smell of fresh meat, and he sometimes attacked men, or apparently more often women, on horseback, perhaps in search of horsemeat, of which he was fond. There are recorded instances of his having killed children, and he was thought to regard a nursing baby as an especial delicacy.

I shall call the two panther themes occurring with greatest frequency "The Panther on the Roof" and "The Panther in Pursuit."[14]

---

[11] T. B. Thorpe, "The Big Bear of Arkansas," in *Tall Tales of the Southwest,* edited by Franklin J. Meine (New York, 1930), p. 16.

[12] Adam Lawrence came to the Red River Valley in 1815, and joined Austin's colony in 1822. Stories about his adventures were written, some in the first person, by W. S. Wade, before Lawrence's death in 1878. A typescript of Wade's work, entitled "Tales of Early Texas," has been furnished me by John Poindexter Landers, a great-grandson of Lawrence.

[13] The elk were evidently thrown in for good measure. They are not native to Texas.

[14] Two versions of the "The Panther on the Roof" and five versions of "The Panther in Pursuit" may be found in J. Frank Dobie, *Tales of Old Time Texas* (Boston, 1955), pp. 181-94. Dobie has others in his files.

My example of the first is from the Glimp family saga.[15] The Glimp family went on a bear hunt to lay in a supply of meat for winter, Sarah and her three-month-old baby along with the men-folks. Near where they expected to find bear, they built a log hut with a fireplace and clay-daubed chimney. They laid a roof of unspecified material on pole rafters. The men cut and brought in a supply of firewood, and left Sarah with her baby and a hound while they went to look for bear.

During the afternoon the baby began crying from colic. At dusk it was still crying. As Sarah got up to close the door, she heard a panther scream. He screamed three times, each time sounding nearer. Then she heard him near the door, his snarls answered by the growls and barks of the dog. The next sound she heard was the thud of the panther's landing on the roof, which sagged under his weight as he walked. The baby cried and the dog barked. The panther walked toward the chimney. She knew it was large enough for him to come through. She started piling wood on the fire, and kept piling it on until she noticed that the clay was cracking. If it fell and exposed the sticks, the cabin would burn down. Her problem was to keep just the right amount of heat going up the chimney. Eventually the baby went to sleep. She put him on a pallet and seated herself by the fire with a knife in her hand. She was still sitting there awake when the men returned next morning.

With the dog they soon found the panther not more than a hundred yards away, and shot it. Although the hound was well trained and had always been obedient, he leaped upon the panther as it fell from the tree and could not be called away until he had completely ruined the hide.[16]

The motif of the panther in pursuit is essentially that of the fairy tale in which the hero, pursued by an ogre, drops objects

---

[15] J. D. Brantley, "Reminiscences of a Texas Pioneer," unpublished manuscript.

[16] On whether the event happened before or after the family moved from Tennessee to Texas in 1822, Sarah Glimp's descendants are not agreed.

which become obstacles to slow down the pursuer. The objects, however, are not bottles of water that become great lakes or twigs that become dense forests.

When J. Frank Dobie was a boy he used to hear a neighbor tell of a turkey hunt he once had. Taking his shotgun, for which he discovered he had only two loads, he got on his horse late one afternoon and rode toward a turkey roost. About a half-mile from the roost he came to a fence. There he tied his horse and walked on. He hid and waited for the turkeys to settle down and for the moon to rise. In the moonlight he aimed at several turkeys lined up on a limb and fired both barrels. Six turkeys fell. He was carrying them toward his horse when he heard a panther scream right behind him. He dropped one of the turkeys and ran as fast as he could. He had not gone far when the panther screamed again. He dropped another turkey. He dropped the last one just in time to leap on his plunging horse as the panther screamed again.

Dobie used to wonder what would have happened if the man had killed only five turkeys or if his horse had been a mile away instead of a half-mile. It was not till years later that he learned that the story had been "told for generations in many localities, pieces of venison or other game sometimes substituting for the dropped turkeys."[17]

Sometimes the substitute is articles of clothing, and the person in flight is a woman, with or without a baby. She is riding in a vehicle or on horseback, when a panther screams and gives chase. Purposely or accidentally she drops her scarf or the baby's cap. The panther, attracted by the human scent, stops and smells and nuzzles the article of clothing, giving the woman a chance to get ahead. But he is soon coming again faster than the fastest horse can run. She drops another garment. She may strip the baby before she gets home, but no version has come to my attention in which she had to twitch her own last garment off.

Again, as would be expected, the pioneer family saga reflects

[17] Dobie, *op. cit.*, pp. 183-84.

the conflicts with the Indians, but here again it is selective. An Indian attack on a settlement or a party of hunters, where little happens except that men on both sides get killed, survives as an item of history. It survives in documents and books, but not in the folk memory. The event will pass into the oral tradition only when there is some added interest.

Sometimes this interest is comic, as in the story of the slow mule. The version that follows is from the Adam Lawrence saga. As Wade had the story, the Indians stole nearly all the horses in the settlement, and Lawrence organized a mustang hunt to replace them. Soon after the party had made camp the first night, a man named Jim Jones rode up on a long-legged mule and begged to join them. Lawrence told him that that would be impossible, for they were going into Indian country and might have to run for their lives. "If that happened," he said, "the Indians would sure catch you on that mule and scalp you."

Jones insisted, however, and was finally permitted to go at his own risk. One day when he and Lawrence were scouting for mustangs some distance from the camp, where pens had been built, they topped a hill and saw about forty Comanches in war paint and feathers not more than six hundred yards away, coming toward them. The Indians raised a war whoop and charged. The two white men made a run for camp. They kept well ahead of the Indians for three or four miles. Then the mule began to "throw up his tail." Lawrence begged Jones to leave the mule and get up behind him, but Jones refused, saying the horse could not carry two men and both would be killed. He gave his watch to Lawrence, asking him to send it to his mother and tell her that nobody was to blame but him. This seemed final and there was no time for further parley. Lawrence rode on.

Two or three minutes afterwards [Wade has him say] I heard an awful screeching and yelling, and my heart came in my mouth, for I thought they was scalping Jim. But they weren't, for just then I heard a pat, pat right behind me, and I whirled back with my rifle gun cocked, for I thought it was an Indian; but I saw it was Jim, and you ought to have seen that mule, as it passed by me almost like I was standing still. Its nose was sticking straight out and smoke was a-coming out of it like steam out of a kettle. Its ears was laid back on its neck like they was pinned back. Its tail was a-sticking out behind him and it looked like he was jumping forty feet at a time. I noticed three arrows sticking up in that mule's rump. As Jim passed me he hollered back and said, "Farewell, Ad." What was them Indians yelling about? Why they was watching that mule fly. They turned back north.

When I got to camp the boys were behind trees with their guns ready, but I told them that them Indians wouldn't follow us in the timber, for they knowed when we shot we got meat. Jim had his saddle off trying to pull the arrows out of his mule. I roped his fore feet and throwed it and cut them out. I was a little careless when I let it up, for it made a bulge and away it went, looking back to where it had been introduced to the Indians. We never saw hide or hair of it again.[18]

The story of the scalping of Josiah Wilbarger, as will be apparent, is a complex one, combining a number of motifs. In August, 1833, Wilbarger was with a surveying party near where the city of Austin is now. At that time the only settlers in the region were Reuben Hornsby and his family and retainers. Six miles from Hornsby's house the surveyors were attacked in camp by Indians. Two men were mortally wounded. One after another Wilbarger's legs were pierced by arrows. The two unwounded men ran for their horses, Wilbarger following after them as best he could. They had mounted when they saw him fall, shot in the back of the neck with a gun. They left him for dead and rode full speed to Hornsby's.

Wilbarger did not lose consciousness, but he knew that his chances of staying alive depended upon his playing dead. This he did successfully, even while the Indians stripped him of all

---

[18] On Lawrence see note 12. John Duval has a version of this story in *The Young Explorers*, first published serially in 1870-71, and in *Early Times in Texas* (Austin, 1892), pp. 150-54. His principal characters are Uncle Seth and Bill Shanks, rather than Lawrence and Jones, and his mule is not hit by the Indians' arrows.

his clothing but one sock, and scalped him. When the scalp was torn from his head, he experienced no sharp pain, but heard a loud noise like thunder.

Then he lost consciousness. When he regained it he was alone. He dragged himself to the creek, rolled into the water and drank and rested. Becoming chilled, he crawled out and lay in the sun. Later he went back to the creek, drank, ate some snails, and began crawling in the direction of the Hornsby cabins. Exhausted, he lay down with his head against a tree.

As he lay there, a form, which he recognized as that of his sister, Margaret Clifton, who lived in Missouri, appeared and said, "Brother Josiah, you are too weak to go by yourself. Remain here, and friends will come and take care of you before the setting of the sun." When she had said this she moved away in the direction of the Hornsby place.

The men who had escaped reported Wilbarger dead. They had seen him fall with fifty Indians swarming around him. That night Mrs. Hornsby woke from a dream, called her husband and told him that Wilbarger was still alive. In her dream she had seen him wounded, naked, and scalped, but alive. Reuben Hornsby, thinking that his wife's nerves had been overwrought by the events of the day, calmed her and told her to go back to sleep. She did, only to be awakened by the same dream, the image of Wilbarger by the tree.

This time she got up, made coffee, and would not let the men rest until they promised to go to Wilbarger's relief at daybreak.

At the time of his rescue Wilbarger told of the apparition of his sister. Mails were slow in those days, and it was not until a month later that he got a letter from Missouri bringing the news of his sister's death on the day before he was wounded. He lived eleven years longer and his descendants still tell his story without significant variation.[19] A text has been in print

---

[19] The story as told by Wilbur C. Gilbert, a grandson of Josiah Wilbarger, was tape recorded July 23, 1953. Gilbert mislocates the Hornsby

since 1889,[20] which no doubt has militated against change. Yet one wonders how as a folk tale it could be improved.

The first chronicler, puzzled by the event he had recounted, concluded: "We leave to those more learned the task of explaining the visions of Wilbarger and Mrs. Hornsby. It must remain a marvel and a mystery."[21]

There is no marvel or mystery in the incredible. In most segments of our population the ghost story survives only as a quaint relic of the past. It will not be a part of the living folklore unless it is both marvelous and believable. The Wilbarger story passes this test, as do a few others. A college student has recently written:

When the writer's great-grandmother was a young girl in her early teens, she attended a slumber party given by one of the neighbors, at which about ten girls were present. Even in those days none of the guests slept at a slumber party. As the night wore on, the conversation turned to ghosts, ghost stories, and cemeteries. All but one girl admitted they would be afraid to go to a cemetery at night. The one girl held fast to her boast that she was afraid of nothing, not even ghosts. The other girls called her bluff and double-dared her to go to the Liberty Grove cemetery, which was about a mile and a half away. She took the dare; and to prove that she had fulfilled her mission, she was to take a knife and stick it in the grave of a person they all knew who had recently passed on. She took the knife and slipped out of the house.

Next morning she was found stretched across the grave, her face frozen in an expression of terror. The hem of her skirt was pinned to the grave by the knife.[22]

The old dream-book lore seems to be gone. People who dream of a death no longer expect a wedding, and people who dream of muddy water no longer expect a death. Nor has a Freudian

---

ranch by about twenty miles, a fact that would indicate that he had not recently read the published version.

[20] J. W. Wilbarger, *Indian Depredations in Texas* (Austin, 1889), pp. 2-13.

[21] Gilbert, *op. cit.*

[22] Maurita Russell Lueg, "Russell Tales," unpublished manuscript.

symbolism supplanted the old. Dreams that get into the family sagas are, like Mrs. Hornsby's, direct and obvious in their meaning.

A recent example concerns the Rust family, formerly of Ranger. As John Rust tells the story after hearing it from his parents "a countless number of times," his mother awoke one morning and said, "Jim, we'll never sell this little farm. Regardless of what happens, we'll hold on to it as long as we live."

He said, "Why, Mary, do you feel that way about it all of a sudden?"

She said, "Last night I had a dream. Look out this kitchen window, up here at this side of the hill, will you, just a hundred feet away? See that old live-oak tree out there, the largest tree on our place?"

He said, "Yes, what about it?"

"Well, right there under that tree is where we will find our fortune, because in my dream last night it was very vivid — the picture of that tree — and our fortune will be found right there under that tree. Now in what form my dream did not let me know, but I know . . . that that dream was more than a dream — it was a vision."[23]

In 1915 a neighbor of the Rusts named Jim Baker, "who had become famous in that section of the country for locating water wells with a peach-tree limb," came to the Rust home and said he had always had a feeling that there was silver upon the hill, and asked permission to prospect there. Jim Rust told him to go ahead — he could have half of all the silver he found. Baker cut a fork from a peach tree, tied a dime to it and began walking over the farm. The peach fork turned down and came to rest under the tree of Mrs. Rust's dream. Baker showed up the next day with an auger and began boring by hand. At about a hundred feet, however, he gave up hope and quit.

Two years later oil was discovered on the adjoining McClesky farm, and the Texas and Pacific Coal and Oil Company leased

---

[23] From a tape-recorded interview with John Rust, Borger, Texas, September 15, 1952.

the Rust farm. Two days later workmen came and cut down the big live oak in order to make room for the drilling rig. The well came in, making ten thousand barrels a day.

"I guess there might be something in dreams," concludes John Rust. "There was something in that dream. The fortune was there just like the dream told my mother years before."[24]

There can be found in Texas, however, a considerable number of families whose total wealth is less than a million dollars. Of these a considerable number sometime in the past have barely missed getting rich. If it was in this century, the fortune would have been made in oil. Father or grandfather had a farm or a ranch or some timberland a mile or two or three from a newly introduced wildcat well producing X thousand barrels a day. Various producers wanted to lease his land. They bid the price up to X thousand dollars an acre. But father or grandfather held out for more. In the meantime a well was going down between the discovery well and his land. It was dry.

Or, a small independent wildcatter was poorboying a well. At fifteen hundred feet his last dollar was gone. He went to father or grandfather and offered him a large interest in the venture for enough cash to drill another five hundred feet. Father or grandfather had the money idle in the bank, but the proposition looked too risky. He declined. The wildcatter found the money somewhere else and struck oil before he had gone another hundred feet.

If it was in the nineteenth century that the ancestor missed the fortune, he missed it by failing to find a lost mine or buried treasure. This was the experience of Adam Lawrence. In 1833 when he was living on a ranch west of the Brazos, an old Spaniard walked up to his cabin one day and said he was sick and needed help. Lawrence cared for him until he was well. Then the Spaniard told him that he had been a member of Lafitte's pirate crew, and that when his master was captured, he and two others were guarding the treasure on Galveston Island

---

[24] *Ibid.*

some distance from the scene of surrender. They placed the treasure in two small cannon, the gold in one and the silver in the other, and buried them in the sand 703 varas from a hackberry tree. They took an oath that none of them would try to recover the treasure unless all three were present. They made their escapes, going in different directions.

The Spaniard had recently learned that the other two were dead. Released from his oath, he was on his way to dig up the cannon. If Lawrence would go with him and help him, he would give him half the treasure, and if he would take care of him the rest of his life, he would make him his heir.

On their way to Galveston Island, they camped on November 3. That was the night the stars fell on Texas. In the bright moonlight Lawrence observed the old Spaniard asleep with his shirt open. There was a great scar on his chest. His relaxed face looked inhuman. An owl hooted in a nearby bottom; a timber wolf howled. Lawrence began to wonder. Maybe the old man was the devil leading him to destruction.

All at once the heavens seemed to be on fire; shooting stars were falling all around. Lawrence sprang on his horse and fled for home. He reached it late the next day, exhausted.

About a month later a man came hunting Lawrence. He said that the old Spaniard had died at his cabin a few days after the stars fell, and had given him a package to be delivered to "Señor" Lawrence. The package contained a map of Galveston Island, showing a hackberry tree and a line leading from it marked 703 varas. This Lawrence gave to his wife Sallie, telling her to put it away carefully. He then wrote his brother-in-law, Lindsay Rucker, a surveyor, to join him. But when Rucker arrived Sallie had forgotten where she put the map. They proceeded without it, but found nothing. Many years later a cannon filled with silver was washed up during a storm. The gold must still be there.[25]

If your name is Duarte or Guerra, your family saga will bear

---

[25] Wade, *op. cit.*

a resemblance to those of the Smiths and the Lawrences. There will perhaps be more emphasis on the supernatural.

It might well include a tale about how the jumping about of the stove led an ancestor to suspect the presence of a ghost; how he consulted his *compadre* as one more learned in such things than he; how the *compadre* concluded that without doubt a ghost was trying to reveal the hiding place of a treasure and that whoever found it must pay the debts of the deceased so that his spirit might have rest; how when the two men were digging under the stove, a voice said, "Whoever takes my fortune takes my debts also"; how they uncovered a chest full of gold; how the *compadre* took it all, promising to pay the ghost's debts and give the other man half the remainder; how when a week had passed and no debts had been paid, the *compadre* was found dead, his mouth full of mud; and how when the chest was opened it contained nothing but mud.[26]

Or your family might include a story, as that of the Guerra family does, about the Texas Rangers, *"los rinches"* of the Mexican Border ballads. The Guerras stood for law and order during a long period of international banditry — a banditry in which citizens of both republics were involved, and one which reached a climax during the Civil War and Reconstruction. When Texas was readmitted to the Union, the Ranger force was reorganized and sent to the Border with emphatic orders to suppress crime. Using methods other than passive resistance, they were largely though not wholly successful.

It was during this time that Uncle Pedro Fulano was living on a ranch he had established some miles from Buena Vista, the Guerra home. One day Uncle Pedro missed some horses. He followed their tracks and about nightfall came to a camp where three men had them in their possession. When he demanded his property, they opened fire. Unhit, he fired back. He killed one man and the other two fled. He took his horses home and the

---

[26] Guadalupe Duarte, "Around the Fire with My Abuelitos," unpublished manuscript.

next day rode to the county seat, reported what he had done, and
demanded a trial. He was acquitted.

About a month later two Rangers stopped at the Guerra
ranch and asked how they might find Pedro Fulano. They said
they wanted to congratulate him upon the bravery he had dis-
played in the protection of his property. Their host, somewhat
suspicious at first, became convinced of their good faith, but he
knew that Pedro would probably be alarmed. He told one of
his sons to saddle a horse and ride immediately to Uncle Pedro's
and prepare him for the visit. In the meantime he insisted
that the Rangers stay for supper.

When they reached Uncle Pedro's ranch, he was not there.
Two weeks later his wife got a letter saying that he was safe in
Mexico. He had found a suitable location, and she was to sell
the ranch and join him.

Uncle Pedro's story is told on the Border. It shows how the
barbaric *"rinches"* terrified even honest men.[27]

I have attempted by examples to indicate the kind of folklore
found in the family saga. Since most of these stories exist in
multiple versions and are attached to more than one person, they
cannot all be true. A study of the migration of specific stories
might be undertaken when more versions are available.

In the meantime the fact of their migration from place to
place and from person to person is not difficult to account for.

Listeners, especially children, often confuse narrator and
actor. When I was a child, for example, my mother told me the
story of the trapped corn thief. This tale concerns a man who,
seeing that corn was being taken through a crack in his crib at
night, set a steel trap and chained it inside the crib. The next
morning he saw a neighbor standing with his hand in the crack.
"Good morning, Mr. Blank," he said; "come in and have
breakfast."

When I told a neighbor boy how my grandfather had caught
a thief in a steel trap, he said it wasn't my grandfather at all.

---

[27] Fermina Guerra, *Mexican and Spanish Folklore and Incidents in
Southwest Texas* (Master's thesis, University of Texas, 1941), pp. 36-38.

The tale was old hat to him. I questioned my mother and she explained that she had said her father *told* the story. She had *not* said that he was the one who set the trap. Later I was to find the story widely diffused.

Again, characters who are vivid for whatever reason attract stories. One has only to recall such historical personages as Andrew Jackson, Sam Houston, and Abe Lincoln of Illinois — or Peter Cartwright, also of Illinois, who once complained that "almost all those various incidents that had gained currency throughout the country, concerning Methodist preachers, had been located on me."[28]

Finally the very art of narration encourages attribution to persons the narrator knows or knows about. One cannot say, "A told me that B told him that C told him that D told him that E went on a turkey hunt." If the age and known experience of the narrator are such that he can plausibly say, "I went on a turkey hunt," that is what he is likely to say. Or if he is too young, "My father [or Uncle John, or Grandfather] went on a turkey hunt."

I have chosen my examples from Texas because that is where my work has chiefly been done. But I should like to suggest to folklorists all over America that in the family saga we have an important source of living folklore — a folklore that can be collected with relative ease. Each generation produces a few collectors and raconteurs of the family lore. These can be found and encouraged to talk, sometimes into microphones. Teachers in colleges and universities can put their students to work. Young Americans, like their elders, are searching for a past. They will bring you much chaff but more than enough wheat to compensate for it. Some students get a keen emotional satisfaction in questioning elderly friends and relatives and writing their family lore. If they feel secure in their status they will be honest. They will even tell you the Illinois equivalent of why great-great-great-grandfather came to Texas.

---

[28] Peter Cartwright, *Autobiography* (New York, 1856), p. 109.

ROBERT B. DOWNS

APOCRYPHAL BIOLOGY:
A CHAPTER IN AMERICAN FOLKLORE

Broadly interpreted, American folklore has a spread and sweep comparable to our national culture. A full understanding of our way of life could hardly be gained without an appreciation of our oral traditions.

One of the most extraordinary and fascinating chapters of the American folklore heritage relates to animal, insect, and plant life. Our creations dealing with natural history surpass all others in vivid flights of fancy, inventiveness, humor, and originality. As Ben Clough put it, "From Maine to Idaho, from the Adirondacks to Arkansas, unlikely creatures crawl, prowl, whine, and roar through the jungles of America's imagination."[1]

Any professional folklorist will readily concede that little of our folklore is strictly indigenous, except that of the American Indian, which was here when the white man came. As a people we share the common inheritance of English and Old World culture. This is not to suggest, however, that the folk traditions of the past have remained unchanged in the New World. To the folklore which the settlers brought with them from their home countries have been added experiences and impressions to blend

---

[1] Ben C. Clough, "Wonders of Nature," in his *The American Imagination at Work* (New York, 1947), pp. 133-222.

with their inherited background. Nowhere is this point better illustrated than in the field of biology.

Animal mythology is, of course, as ancient as and probably much older than written literature.[2] Aesop in his *Fables* told of talking animals, and Pliny's *Natural History* described dolphins carrying human riders. In every period of literature mythological creatures abound. The dragon, with its lion's claws, eagle's wings, serpent's tail, and fiery breath, has persisted from Babylonian times down through Chinese lore, the medieval Nibelungenlied, Beowulf, and the story of St. George. The griffin, a cross between a lion and an eagle, originated with the Hittites and came on down through the Assyrians and the Persians to medieval times. The unicorn, a monster with a long horn jutting from the middle of its forehead, with the legs of an antelope and the body of a horse, was probably created in India, but recurs frequently in the mythology of other countries and races. Centaurs, part man and part horse, Pegasus, a winged horse, and the chimera, a fire-breathing monster, appeared in Greek mythology. Do these seem much more incredible than the duckbilled, egg-laying mammal known as the platypus?

In view of these awe-inspiring and terrifying beasts out of past ages, it cannot be claimed that unnatural natural history was born in America, but there is no doubt that it has flourished mightily in our fertile soil. To match the fabulous fauna of the Old World, such amazing animals as the hodag, the whifflepoofle, the sidehill gouger, the squonk, the cactus cat, the dingmaul, the gumberoo, the hoop-snake, the wampus, and the swamp auger may be offered.

America is and always has been a land of magnificent stories, both true and false. To the early pioneer little or nothing seemed impossible. The wild frontier produced mighty boasters, and bold men created bold myths. It is probable that our natural-history folklore was stimulated by the totally different flora and fauna of the New World. One can imagine how these must have

---

[2] Peter Lum, *Fabulous Beasts* (New York, 1951).

affected pioneers from the Old World. Van Wyck Brooks, writing of "the wondrous West" in the period around 1800, offered these discerning comments:

One heard of watermelons as large as houses and trees on the Miami River in which honey grew, springs of rum and brandy that gushed from the Kentucky hills and flax-plants that bore woven cloth in their branches. With these humorous yarns were mingled others that might have been true; and how was a credulous Easterner to draw the line? Was there not really perhaps a hoop-snake that spun through the swamps like a wheel, a whip-snake that killed cattle with the lashing of its tail and a serpent that exhaled a fatal gas? These tall tales that crossed the mountains were true as intimations that almost anything indeed might happen in the West.[3]

American natural-history folklore is of two types. The first concerns improbable behavior on the part of known animals, insects, or plants; the second, the actions of mythical beasts. It will be my purpose to demonstrate both varieties.

Possibly the father of apocryphal biology as well as of the tall tale in America was Benjamin Franklin. In 1765, satirizing the ignorance of Englishmen regarding the New World, Dr. Franklin wrote: "The very tails of the American sheep are so laden with wool, that each has a little car or wagon on four little wheels, to support and keep it from trailing on the ground." Warming to his task, Franklin continued, "Cod, like other fish when attacked by their enemies, fly into any waters where they can be safest; Whales when they have a mind to eat Cod, pursue them wherever they fly; and the grand leap of the Whale in that chase up Niagara Falls is esteemed, by all who have seen it, as one of the finest spectacles in nature."[4]

On second thought, however, perhaps Christopher Columbus deserves first priority in the tall tale–natural history department,

---

[3] Van Wyck Brooks, *The World of Washington Irving* (New York, 1944), p. 115.

[4] Harold W. Thompson, *Body, Boots and Britches* (Philadelphia, 1940), p. 128.

on the basis of his report after returning home that "at a distance there were men with one eye only, and others with faces like dogs, who were man-eaters," a whopper that he picked up from the Indians of Haiti.[5]

The state of scientific knowledge and the credulousness of our colonial ancestors are indicated further by an incident reported as fact by Cotton Mather in 1712 to the Royal Society of London. As printed in the Society's *Philosophical Transactions,* Mather wrote: "A Person provoking a Rattle-Snake to bite the Edge of a broad Axe he had in his Hand; the colour, of the Steeled part bitten, was immediately changed, and at the first stroke he made with it in using his Ax, the so discoloured part broke out, leaving a gap in his Ax."[6]

In the category of abnormal behavior among recognized members of the animal kingdom belong some of the most exhilarating and hilarious examples of American folk tales. These, of course, are descended from a long line, with such legitimate antecedents in the Old World as the inventions of Sir John Mandeville in the fourteenth century and of Baron Munchausen in the eighteenth century.

Of all creations of this nature my own favorite is "Jim Baker's Blue Jay Yarn," as related by Mark Twain. This extravagant concoction was told to Twain by Jim Gillis, a California miner with whom he camped for several months. The story attributes to the blue jay practically all human characteristics, including the ability to talk. It goes as follows:

When I first begun to understand jay language correctly, there was a little incident happened here. Seven years ago, the last man in this region but me moved away. There stands his house, — been empty ever since; a log house, with a plank roof — just one big room, and no more; no ceiling — nothing between the rafters and the floor. Well, one Sunday morning I was sitting out here in

---

[5] Christopher Columbus, *Journal of First Voyage to America* (New York, 1924), p. 60.

[6] Royal Society of London, *Philosophical Transactions,* XXIX (April-June, 1714), 68.

front of my cabin, with my cat, taking the sun, and looking at the blue hills, and listening to the leaves rustling so lonely in the trees, and thinking of the home away yonder in the states, that I hadn't heard from in thirteen years, when a bluejay lit on that house, with an acorn in his mouth, and says, "Hello, I reckon I've struck something." When he spoke, the acorn dropped out of his mouth and rolled down the roof, of course, but he didn't care; his mind was all on the thing he had struck. It was a knot-hole in the roof. He cocked his head to one side, shut one eye and put the other one to the hole, like a 'possum looking down a jug; then he glanced up with his bright eyes, gave a wink or two with his wings — which signifies gratification, you understand, — and says, "It looks like a hole, it's located like a hole, — blamed if I don't believe it *is* a hole!"

Then he cocked his head down and took another look; he glances up perfectly joyful, this time; winks his wings and his tail both, and says, "Oh, no, this ain't no fat thing, I reckon! If I ain't in luck! — why it's a perfectly elegant hole!" So he flew down and got that acorn, and fetched it up and dropped it in, and was just tilting his head back, with the heavenliest smile on his face, when all of a sudden he was paralyzed into a listening attitude and that smile faded gradually out of his countenance like breath off'n a razor, and the queerest look of surprise took its place. Then he says, "Why, I didn't hear it fall!" He cocked his eye at the hole again, and took a long look; raised up and shook his head; stepped around to the other side of the hole and took another look from that side; shook his head again. He studied a while, then he just went into the *de*tails — walked round and round the hole and spied into it from every point of the compass. No use. Now he took a thinking attitude on the comb of the roof and scratched the back of his head with his right foot a minute, and finally says, "Well, it's too many for *me,* that's certain; must be a mighty long hole; however, I ain't got no time to fool around here, I got to 'tend to business; I reckon it's all right — chance it, anyway."

So he flew off and fetched another acorn and dropped it in, and tried to flirt his eye to the hole quick enough to see what become of it, but he was too late. He held his eye there as much as a minute; then he raised up and sighed, and says, "Confound it,

I don't seem to understand this thing, no way; however, I'll tackle her again." He fetched another acorn, and done his level best to see what become of it, but he couldn't. He says, "Well, *I* never struck no such a hole as this before; I'm of the opinion it's a totally new kind of a hole." Then he begun to get mad. He held in for a spell, walking up and down the comb of the roof and shaking his head and muttering to himself; but his feelings got the upper hand of him, presently, and he broke loose and cussed himself black in the face. I never see a bird take on so about a little thing. When he got through he walks to the hole and looks in again for half a minute; then he says, "Well, you're a long hole, and a deep hole, and a mighty singular hole altogether — but I've started in to fill you, and I'm d — d if I *don't* fill you, if it takes a hundred years!"

And with that, away he went. You never see a bird work so since you was born. He laid into his work like a nigger, and the way he hove acorns into that hole for about two hours and a half was one of the most exciting and astonishing spectacles I ever struck. He never stopped to take a look any more — he just hove 'em in and went for more. Well, at last he could hardly flop his wings, he was so tuckered out. He comes a-drooping down, once more, sweating like an ice-pitcher, drops his acorn in and says, "*Now* I guess I've got the bulge on you by this time!" So he bent down for a look. If you'll believe me, when his head come up again he was just pale with rage. He says, "I've shoveled acorns enough in there to keep the family thirty years, and if I can see a sign of one of 'em I wish I may land in a museum with a belly full of sawdust in two minutes!"

He just had strength enough to crawl up on to the comb and lean his back agin the chimbly, and then he collected his impressions and begun to free his mind. I see in a second that what I had mistook for profanity in the mines was only just the rudiments, as you may say.

Another jay was going by, and heard him doing his devotions, and stops to inquire what was up. The sufferer told him the whole circumstance, and says, "Now yonder's the hole, and if you don't believe me, go and look for yourself." So this fellow went and looked, and comes back and says, "How many did you say you put in there?" "Not any less than two tons," says the sufferer. The other jay went and looked again. He couldn't seem to make it out, so he raised a yell, and three more jays come. They all examined the hole, they all made the sufferer tell it over again, then they all discussed it, and got off as many leather-headed opinions about it as an average crowd of humans could have done.

They called in more jays; then more and more, till pretty soon this whole region 'peared to have a blue flush about it. There must have been five thousand of them; and such another jawing and disputing and ripping and cussing, you never heard. Every jay in the whole lot put his eye to the hole and delivered a more chuckle-headed opinion about the mystery than the jay that went there before him. They examined the house all over, too. The door was standing half open, and at last one old jay happened to go and light on it and look in. Of course, that knocked the mystery galley-west in a second. There lay the acorns, scattered all over the floor. He flopped his wings and raised a whoop. "Come here!" he says, "Come here, everybody; hang'd if this fool hasn't been trying to fill up a house with acorns!" They all came a-swooping down like a blue cloud, and as each fellow lit on the door and took a glance, the whole absurdity of the contract that that first jay had tackled hit him home and he fell over backwards suffocating with laughter, and the next jay took his place and done the same.

Well, sir, they roosted around here on the housetop and the trees for an hour, and guffawed over that thing like human beings. It ain't any use to tell me a bluejay hasn't got a sense of humor, because I know better. And memory, too. They brought jays here from all over the United States to look down that hole, every summer for three years. Other birds, too. And they could all see the point, except an owl that come from Nova Scotia to visit the Yo Semite, and he took this thing in on his way back. He said he couldn't see anything funny in it. But then he was a good deal disappointed about Yo Semite, too.[7]

We see in the "Blue Jay Yarn" an age-old tendency of man to create animals in his own image. It is a pleasant conceit to imagine animals with the power of speech and men who have

---

[7] Mark Twain, "Jim Baker's Blue Jay Yarn," in his *A Tramp Aboard* (Author's National Edition, New York, 1907), pp. 24-32.

the power to understand the language of birds and beasts. This explains the antiquity and universality of such animal tales from Aesop and Balaam's ass to Rudyard Kipling's *Jungle Books,* Uncle Remus' Br'er Rabbit, and Don Marquis' Archy and Mehitabel.

Extraordinary behavior is not confined to the zoological branch of natural history. The botanical likewise has its amazing fables. Tales abound concerning giant pumpkins, potatoes, watermelons, corn, and other products of the farm. Again, however, my first choice is a story entitled "Uncle Heber's Flytrap," recorded some years ago in eastern North Carolina. The two principal characters are the laziest man in the state and the plant known as Venus's-flytrap, described by Charles Darwin as "one of the most wonderful plants in the world."

There ain't no question 'bout my ole Uncle Heber being the goldurnest laziest man in these parts, I reckon. Spent his full life trying to hatch up new ways of gitting outen work. Lots of folks 'cused him of shirking his dooties, and when he didn't make no comeback they said he didn't have no shame even, but I reckon the truth is he jes didn't have no energy to make argyment.

He never took no wife 'cause he was too lazy to go courting; and doing his own housekeeping like he done, he jes nacherly let his place go to rack and ruin. The shingles of his house all blowed off, and part of the roof caved in. Cracks come in the walls, and it rained in so hard that ever'thing in the house was wet. Uncle Heber stuck it out until the cracks got so big that the wind'd come in and blow the civers offen his bed. He caught cold and almost died 'cause he was too lazy to sneeze, even. At last the house sorta give up and caved in, and then Uncle Heber knowed he's got to move sommers else.

Feller told him 'bout a little island, eight mile up Brice's Crick, what nobody claimed, and Uncle Heber jes moved on up there. Was too lazy to explore it first, jes put his stuff together in a duffel bag, called his dog, and off he set.

The ground on that island was the richest, I reckon, anywhere could be found. No crops had ever been growed on it and it was made up of silt washed up from the crick. Uncle Heber was in the best piece of luck anybody ever heerd of, I reckon. All he had to do was push a stick in the ground, and goldurn if it didn't take root and grow. On the island was enormous trees of all kinds, some of 'em as thick in the trunk as a house. They was apple trees with apples as big as punkins, and persimmon trees with persimmons as big as your head and as sour as a old maid schoolteacher's mouth. The catfish in the crick was as big as alligators. Only trouble was that ever'thing else was in perportion. The good things was the bestest, but the bad things was the worstest anybody ever heerd tell of.

Uncle Heber sure was in clover. He found a big holler tree what he makes into a house, and there's plenty of fruit and fish and ever'thing he needs. He had brung along his old clay pipe and some fine-cut backer, and of course when he filled his pipe he spilt some backer and jest let it lay. Well, the backer took roots and growed up into the biggest and strongest backer leaves anybody ever heerd of.

He figgered out a good way to catch catfish and not tire hisself out. He'd balance his pole on a forked stick, and put a rock on the limb of a tree jes over the shore end of the pole. On the rock he tied a string. Then in the limb of the tree he rigged up a sharp knife atween two tater graters. He'd stretch hisself out on the crick bank, puffing on his pipe and cogerate hisself on how to cut down on his work. When he sees a nibble on the fishline, he pulls the string. The rock falls off on the end of the pole. This jerks the fish outen the water, 'crost the knife what guts it, and through the tater graters what takes off the scales. He didn't bother 'bout the heads and tails, jes cooked the fish thataway and left the rest for his dog.

Uncle Heber'd lost all his teeth when he was a young feller, jes 'cause he was too lazy to chew his food, I reckon, but he got 'round that all right. He traded a man outen a set of store teeth and then rigged up some clockwork to make the teeth champ up and down. Uncle Heber'd wind up the clockwork and put them in his mouth and let his jaw hang loose. Then he'd feed in his rations and the teeth'd chew it up for him. He used to keep the teeth in his hip pocket, but oncet they got started running in his pocket and bit a hunk outen Uncle Heber, and after that he kept 'em out on the table where he could see 'em.

Oncet he was laying on his back 'longside his fishpole on the crick bank, smoking his pipe and figgering how he was getting tired of catfish and wanted some fresh meat and how he could get some meat without trubble, when a big idee hit him. He 'membered 'bout a little plant he'd seen down near Wilmin'ton what folks call the Venus flytrap and this plant catches flies and little frogs. He figgered that in his fertile land mebbe one of them flytraps'd grow big enough to trap him some game.

After worrying 'bout it two or three months, he got up enough energy to push his raft acrost the crick, walk to the road, and pick up a ride to Wilmin'ton. He got a Venus plant and took it back to his island and planted it in a clear space.

In no time atall that plant begin to grow, and Uncle Heber see he had figgered proper and correct and the plant is going to be big as a live-oak tree. When the Venus plant was six foot high, it caught a rabbit one night. In the morning Uncle Heber see the jaws of the trap shet tight and a rabbit tail sticking out. He figgered and figgered how to git the rabbit out and fin'ly he hit on it. I be goldurn if he didn't light up his pipe with that strong backer and blow at the Venus trap. The plant got real white and began to shiver and opened up its trap and let the rabbit drop out.

Uncle Heber figgered this was the best luck of all. The Venus plant kept on catching him game, most every night, and in a few months it was big enough to catch a deer or a bear. Uncle Heber had so much game he didn't bother to fish no more, jes eat his fill on game. This went on for quite a spell, and Uncle Heber was sitting purty and the only thing he was worrying 'bout was how to find a easy way to dress his game.

Then late one night he was woke up by a awful yammering going on outside. He got up and crawled outen his holler tree, and it was bright moonlight, and he sees his dog chasing a big skunk 'round the Venus tree. The dog was right behind the skunk, but couldn't quite catch it. All a-sudden the tree reaches out one of its traps and grobs up the skunk and the dog in one gulp.

Now Uncle Heber thunk a lot of his dog. It was his onliest friend, and the only thing he could talk to, and he ruther have 'most anything happen to him 'cept lose his dog. So he runs back to his tree house to fetch his pipe so he can blow smoke on the trap and make it open up.

But I reckon that skunk was too goldurn potent for the Venus trap. When Uncle Heber come up, the Venus tree is shaking all over. It shake back and forth and dip up and down. Big gobs of sticky sap, like 'lasses, come oozing out and run down on the ground. First thing Uncle Heber knowed one of the traps dip down and grob him up entire.

The Venus tree keeps on shaking like it's sick to its stummick. Then it gives a powerful lunge and tore itself up by the roots and landed smack in the middle of the crick.

Iffen it hadn't been that Uncle Heber was smoking his pipe when the trap grobbed him he'd a-been a goner, I reckon. The Venus tree started down stream with him in one trap and the dog and the skunk in 'nother, and he jes puffed up a couple good puffs of that pipe and the Venus tree wilted right down in the water and opened up its traps, wide open. Uncle Heber landed in the water, and the skunk and the dog landed in the water, and the three struck off for shore. Uncle Heber smelt the skunk, and the skunk smelt Uncle Heber, and the skunk jes turned 'round and jumped back in the Venus trap.

Uncle Heber was a changed man after that. He moved to town and got a job in a livery stable, and he give up smoking. Said he couldn't stand that sissy stuff they sold in town and called it backer.[8]

Another type of tale popular among the folk concerns family pets. A proper introduction to this category is provided by a yarn credited by Harold W. Thompson, Cornell University folklorist, to John Darling, champion liar of Sullivan County, New York. In John's words:

I got kind of attached to an old sow once, though she caused me some trouble by always snooping around under the barn and getting into the feed-box. One day when I caught her at her tricks, I grabbed up a broom-stick and hit her on the back. I guess I hit harder than I meant to, and it seemed like I broke her back — I never know my own stren'th. Anyway, she couldn't use her hind legs, and I thought for a while I might have to kill her. But I

---

[8] W. C. Hendricks, editor, "Uncle Heber's Flytrap," in *Bundle of Troubles and Other Tarheel Tales* (Durham, N.C., 1943), pp. 127-31.

managed to build a nice two-wheeled truck for her to pull around under her hind-quarters. One day I missed this particular sow and finally decided that she had gone off somewhere to die. But a few months later, up in our grove of oaks I found her, grunting around, picking up acorns, and as nice and fat and friendly as could be. There was thirteen little pigs running around beside her under the trees, and every one of them had a nice little two-wheeled truck under his hind-quarters.[9]

More plausible, though still somewhat improbable, is a family-pet story told by Jay Monaghan, former Illinois State Historian. On a remote Colorado ranch, he related, was an old chap, Tom Blevins, whose wife couldn't take the lonely life and had gone back to town. The only companion left was a cat, "Old Mitts," of which he was very fond. Late one fall, near the beginning of winter, Old Mitts disappeared. The rancher assumed that she had been eaten by the coyotes. He was so provoked that he declared war on the coyotes and started a campaign of extermination. By spring the walls of his cabin were lined with the hides of forty-five coyotes which he had trapped during the winter.

At this time a friend came out from town to see if the old fellow had survived the winter. For some reason, the rancher appeared a little embarrassed when asked about the display of coyote skins. Finally, the facts came out. Old Mitts had disappeared at the start of cold weather, the coyotes had been blamed, and as many as possible of them had been executed for the crime. But then, a few days before the visitor's arrival, the quilts and blankets piled on the rancher's bed had been taken out for their semiannual airing. As they were shaken, Old Mitts fell out. And, as old Tom expressed it, "She was pressed just as pretty as a flower."[10]

Still another somewhat macabre family-pet story originated out in Idaho:

----

[9] Thompson, *op. cit.*, pp. 133-34.

[10] Lloyd Lewis, "Old Mitts" story retold, in *It Takes All Kinds* (New York, 1947), pp. 6-8.

Acme Sulphide came in from his prospect on Caribou Creek, bringing a big cougar to Larry Frazee's taxidermist shop. "Want him skun out and made into a rug?" asked Larry.

"No sir. Stuff him as is. I wouldn't think of walkun on Petronius."

"Why not? Just a cougar, ain't he?"

"Not by your tin horn. He's an institution, that's what he is. When he was just a kitten I ketched him by the mine shaft. Him and Pluto, they was great friends until Petronius growed up. Then one evening when I comes back, why Pluto was gone and Petronius wouldn't eat his supper. I was plumb mad, but I figgered Pluto was gettun old and wasn't so much account nohow. Then, by gum, I missed Mary, the goat. When I missed the last of the chickens and Petronius showed up with feathers in his whiskers, I made up my mind to shoot him. But I got to thinkun how that goat could butt, and the hens wasn't layun anyhow. So I let it go. But I shoulda bumped him then.

"Lydie, she's my old woman — or she was. Partner of my joys and sorrows for forty years. One evening when I gets back she was gone. No sign of her anywhere exceptun one shoe. And Petronius didn't want no supper agin. That got me mad, danged if it didn't, and I went for my gun to blast the varmint. Then I got to thinkun. Lydie wasn't much for looks and besides, she was about to leave me. She was all for hittun the trail, so I puts my gun up."

"Then what happened?"

"Well, last night he jumped me on the trail and took a big hunk right out of me. That was too danged much. So mount him up pretty. He repersents my whole family."[11]

Though not exactly a family pet, a vast amount of folklore has grown up around the razorback hog. Writing for the Texas Folklore Society some twenty years ago, Charles F. Arrowood commented: "The razorback has been as distinctive of the Southern swamps and pine barrens as the long-horned steer has been of Texas. He was a principal support of life in the region of the Dismal Swamp when Byrd and his party ran the dividing line, and he has been an important economic and social factor

---

[11] Vardis Fisher, editor, "A Family Pet," in *Idaho Lore* (Caldwell, Idaho, 1939), p. 117.

in the region ever since. Nothing tougher ever ran on four legs. The razorback may lack the speed of the wolf, the fighting equipment of a wildcat, the strength of a bear, but no wolf, cat or bear can exceed him in ability to absorb punishment and come back for more."[12]

To illustrate these qualities of toughness in razorbacks, Mr. Arrowood narrated this tale:

A farmer was clearing a new ground — grubbing up the stumps laboriously, by hand. A county demonstration agent came by and showed him how easily and cheaply the stumps could be removed by the use of dynamite. The farmer was delighted. He went to the store, bought dynamite, fuse, and caps. Coming home, he dug a hole by a big white-oak stump, set a charge of dynamite under it, lighted the fuse, and went to his house for supper. The fuse went out, but by that time the farmer was clear of the new ground; so he decided to wait until the next morning before lighting it again.

The next morning, early, the farmer's big razorback hog got up and went foraging. He found that stick of dynamite and ate it. Then he saw the farmer about the barn lot and hustled up to see if he could steal a little corn from the mule's breakfast. He broke into the mule's stall, and made for the feed trough. The mule, naturally, kicked at him, and, for the first and last time in his life, connected. The dynamite, at last, went off.

A neighbor heard the explosion and hurried over. He found the owner leaning over the fence of his barn lot, viewing the ruins.

The neighbor heaved a sympathetic sigh. "It looks pretty bad, friend," he said, "pretty bad."

"Yes," said the victim, "it is bad. Killed my mule, wrecked my barn, broke every window out of one side of my house, and, brother, I've got an awful sick hog."

---

[12] Charles F. Arrowood, "There's a Geography of Humorous Anecdotes," in *In the Shadow of History*, edited by J. Frank Dobie and others, Texas Folklore Society Publications, No. 15 (Austin, 1939), pp. 80-81.

Does this story sound farfetched? Here are two Associated Press reports on actual occurrences:

Jacksonville, Florida, March 31 — Patrolman C. P. Bridwell and R. L. Starratt reported today a collision between a 1949 automobile and a 1944 model mule. Added the police: There was $150 damage to the side of the car, no damage to the mule.

Taylorsville, North Carolina — Boyd Adams picked up his .22 rifle and walked out into his mother-in-law's back yard to kill a chicken for dinner. He aimed at a big pullet and fired. Results: A nearby storage building blew to pieces. Window panes in the farm house were blown out. Chimneys were shaken and damaged. Adams was tossed 30 feet. Windows in Taylorsville, two and a half miles away, rattled. The bullet had ricochetted and set off five cases of dynamite in the storage building. It was to have been used for blasting ditches and stumps. The pullet? Unruffled.

Proceeding from real to mythological animals, the most persistent myth in American folklore concerns the hoop-snake. The outstanding characteristic of a hoop-snake is its habit of tucking its tail in its mouth and rolling at incredible speed in pursuit of its prey. In its tail it carries a high-powered venom. To show the strength of this poison, a hoop-snake stung a lumberjack's ax handle. The venom swelled the handle to such dimensions that the lumberjack was able to cut it up into 946 cords of wood. And then the stuff wouldn't burn. Just lay in the stove and hissed.

Without departing too far from reality, a few crossbreeds should be mentioned. There is, for instance, Paul Bunyan's giant mosquitobees, a species developed by crossing mosquitoes with bumblebees. The hybrid was far more dangerous and ferocious than either of its parents. It is likely that mosquitobees are close cousins of the famous bees of Arkansas which are reported to produce twice as much honey as ordinary bees, because they have been crossed with lightning bugs and work night and day.

Another notorious crossbreed is the whickle, a result of the

HOOP-SNAKE

mating of a canary and a bumblebee. Whickles are found in oil fields and have formed an avid taste for petroleum. Consequently, they get the blame when oil wells go dry. A more beneficial creature was developed by the U.S. Signal Corps. By crossing a homing pigeon with a woodpecker, a bird was produced that not only delivers the message but knocks on the door.

One of the celebrated frontier characters was Bigfoot Wallace. As reported by John C. Duval, Bigfoot returned from Texas to his home in Virginia, and there was regaling a young lady with tales of Texas. Said Bigfoot:

I told her there was a varmint in Texas called the Santa Fe, that was still worse than the tarantula, for the best brass band in the country couldn't cure their sting; that the creature had a hundred legs and a sting on every one of them, besides two large stings in its forked tail, and fangs as big as a rattlesnake's. When they sting you with their legs alone, you might possibly live an hour; when with all their stings, perhaps fifteen or twenty minutes; but when they sting and bite you at the same time, you first turn blue, then yellow, and then a beautiful bottle-green, when your hair all falls out, and finger nails drop off, and in five minutes you are as dead as a door nail, in spite of all the doctors in America.

"Oh! My! Mr. Wallace!" said she. "How have you managed to live so long in that horrible country?"

"Why, you see," said I, "with my tarantula boots made of alligator skin, and my centipede hunting-shirt made of tanned rattlesnake hides, I have escaped pretty well; but these don't protect you against the stinging scorpions, cow-killers, and scaly-back chinches, that crawl about at night when you are asleep! The only way to keep them at a distance is to chaw tobacco and drink whiskey, and that is the reason the Temperance Society never flourished much in Texas."

"Oh!" said she, "what a horrible country that must be, where people have to be stung to death, or else chaw tobacco and drink whiskey! I don't know which is the worst."

"Well," said I, "the people out there don't seem to mind it very much; they get used to it after a while. In fact, they seem to rather like it, for they chaw tobacco and drink whiskey even in the winter time, when the cow-killers and stinging lizards are all frozen up!"[13]

If the Bigfoot Wallace story of the Santa Fe has all the ear-

---

[13] John C. Duval, *Adventures of Bigfoot Wallace* (Macon, Ga., 1870), pp. 293-94.

HODAG

marks of a whopper, consider this description by Alan Moorehead of some of the marine life on the Great Barrier Reef of
Australia:

Then, I would see lovely cone-shaped sea shells marked with a
geometric pattern of brown diamonds, which reminded me of a
batiked cloth. A dangerous crablike animal inhabits these. When
his shell is picked up or disturbed, the creature darts out a sting
whose effects are unbearably painful and so poisonous that people
have been instantly killed by it. If you survive the first shock, you
begin to lose your senses, one by one. You grow deaf and blind.
Your whole body becomes paralyzed, and the agony is such that
you have no will to cry out. Victims have died at this stage of the
ordeal. The usual treatment is to inject morphine, which enables
the patient to bear the pain while his body adjusts itself to the
poison. Little else can be done. The stonefish has this same bane-
ful power, but it differs from the crab in that its very appearance
is a warning. It must be the ugliest creature in existence — a

slimy, discolored fiend with a glaring eye, a skin covered with warts, and thirteen quills on its back, each loaded with poison. It lies motionless in shallow pools on the Reef, and if you stumble upon one and are pierced by a quill, paralysis sets in at once. Even if you survive the first shock, the agony will come back again and again in after weeks, like recurring bouts of malaria.[14]

For further details on America's fabulous beasts, particular indebtedness should be acknowledged to the scholarly researches of William T. Cox, author of *Fearsome Creatures of the Lumberwoods*,[15] Henry H. Tryon, author of *Fearsome Critters*,[16] Charles Edward Brown, author of *Paul Bunyan Natural History*,[17] Vance Randolph, tireless collector of Ozark lore,[18] and Professor Mody C. Boatright of Texas.[19] Space will permit only brief descriptions of a few mysterious monsters.

The most famous goes under a variety of names: sidehill gouger, sidehill hoofer, sidehill dodger, mountain stem winder, etc. To avoid confusion, it is preferable to use its scientific name, *Membri-inequalis Declivitatis*. The peculiar thing about the sidehill gouger is its legs. It has two long legs on the downhill side and two short legs on the uphill side. Some have their right legs long and some their right legs short, depending on which way they graze around the mountains. In appearance they are something like a cross between a buffalo and a mountain goat, only much more ferocious. If a person is chased by one he should not run but wait until the sidehill gouger is within a few feet and then take a couple of steps downhill. The gouger can-

---

[14] Alan Moorehead, "The Great Barrier Reef," *New Yorker*, XXIX (August 15, 1953), 38.

[15] William T. Cox, *Fearsome Creatures of the Lumberwoods, With a Few Desert and Mountain Beasts* (Washington, D.C., 1910).

[16] Henry H. Tryon, *Fearsome Critters* (Cornwall, N.Y., 1939).

[17] Charles Edward Brown, *Paul Bunyan Natural History* (Madison, Wis., 1935).

[18] Vance Randolph, "Fabulous Monsters," in his *We Always Lie to Strangers* (New York, 1951), pp. 41-74.

[19] Mody C. Boatright, "Birds and Beasts," in his *Tall Tales from Texas* (Dallas, 1934), pp. 28-39.

SQUONK

not turn without falling and breaking its neck. Vance Randolph reports a certain hollow in Marion County, Arkansas, which is half full of sidehill-hoofer bones, presumably from animals that have lost their balance and fallen to their deaths.[20] The *Membriinequalis Declivitatis* may be found wherever there is hilly or mountainous country.

---

[20] Randolph, *op. cit.*

Another remarkable animal is the cactus cat, scientifically designated as *Felis Spinobiblulosus* or *Cactifelinus Inebrius,* a native of the Southwest. As its name indicates, it lives in cactus country, and is said to be particularly abundant between Prescott and Tucson. Its physical appearance and operations are thus described by Cox:

The cactus cat has thorny hair, the thorns being especially long and rigid on its ears. Its tail is branched and upon its forearms above its front feet are sharp, knifelike blades of bone. With these blades it slashes the base of giant cactus trees, causing the sap to exude. This is done systematically, many trees being slashed in the course of several nights as the cat makes a big circuit. By the time it is back to the place of beginning the sap of the first cactus has fermented into a kind of mescal, sweet and very intoxicating. This is greedily lapped up by the thirsty beast, which soon becomes fiddling drunk, and goes waltzing off in the moonlight, rasping its bony forearms across each other and screaming with delight.[21]

The north woods, from Maine to Wisconsin, is the habitat of a strange creature known as the hodag.[22] The animal's back resembles that of a dinosaur and its long tail has a spearlike end. Sharp spines, one and a half feet apart, line the spinal column. The legs are short and massive and the claws thick and curved. The broad, furrowed forehead is covered with coarse, shaggy hair and there are two large horns. From the wide, muscular mouth, sharp, glistening, white teeth protrude. As might be judged from this description, the hodag is a distressingly ugly animal. It is fully aware of its upsetting appearance, and is given to frequent fits of bitter weeping.

In this respect it is akin to the squonk, a native of Pennsylvania, whose scientific name is *Lacrimacorpus Dissolvens.*[23] The squonk is of a very retiring disposition, generally traveling about at twilight. Because of its misfitting skin, covered with warts

---

[21] Cox, *op. cit.*

[22] Lake Shore Kearney, *The Hodag and Other Tales of the Logging Camps* (Wausau, Wis., 1928).

[23] Cox, *op. cit.*

FILLA-MA-LOO BIRD

and moles, it is always unhappy; in fact, it is said to be the most morbid of beasts. Hunters who are good at tracking are able to follow a squonk by its tear-stained trail, for the animal weeps constantly. When cornered and escape seems impossible, or when surprised and frightened, it may even dissolve itself in tears.

An animal usually seen around construction camps and engineering jobs is the tripodero, known to scientists as *Collapso-femuris Geocatapeltes*. Its physical features include tripod legs and a beak like the muzzle of a gun with a sight on the end. As it goes through the brush it raises and lowers itself to look for game. "Upon seeing a bird or small animal," according to Brown, "it tilts itself to the rear, sights along its beak and lets fly a pellet of clay." A quantity of hardened clay pellets is carried in a cheek pouch. The tripodero is reputed seldom to miss a shot because it is "a deep student of ballistics, and has fine judgment of distance, wind, and drift."[24]

Two curious creatures are reported from the Rocky Mountain region. One is the augerino, a malevolent subterranean animal "whose sole mission in life is to let the water out of irrigation ditches." It is described as an enormous corkscrew-shaped worm. The other is the ratchet owl, a creature that always faces away from the sun. "In early morning, the ratchet owl faces west, but as the sun follows its daily course, the bird must turn its head, and at sunset is facing due east. To prevent undue strain on its neck muscles, this owl is equipped with a ratchet, which permits easy clockwise rotation of its head. At some time during the night, the owl, in preparation for the next day, releases the ratchet, making a fearful noise, and allows its head to return to a west-facing position."[25]

There are some other peculiar birds among our folklore creations. The gillygaloo, for instance, is a hillside plover, which lays square eggs so that they will not roll down steep inclines where it nests. The lumberjacks hardboil these eggs and use them as dice. Another example is the goofus bird, known sometime as the filla-ma-loo bird. Unlike other birds, it always flies backward instead of forward, because, as one old lumberjack explained, "It doesn't give a darn where it's going, it only wants to know where it's been." It also builds its nest upside down.

[24] Brown, *op. cit.*

[25] Ronald L. Ives, "Folklore of Eastern Park, Colorado," *Journal of American Folklore,* LIV (Jan.-June, 1941), 29, 30.

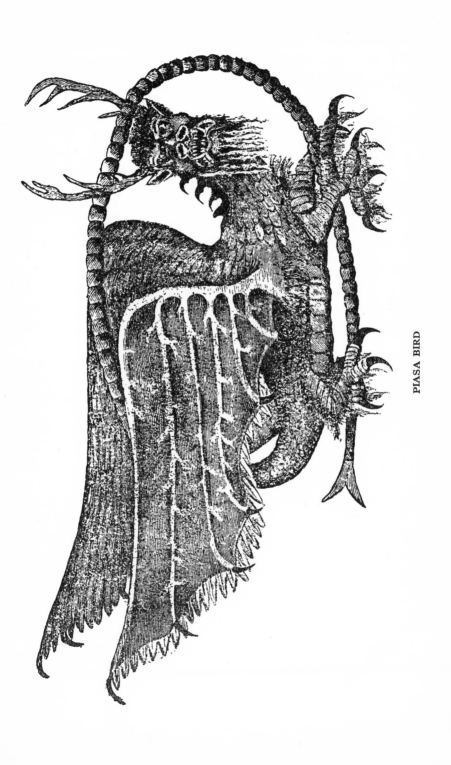

PIASA BIRD

The goofus bird is a relative of the goofang, an odd fish that always swims backward instead of forward. This is to keep the water out of its eyes. The goofang is described as "about the size of a sunfish, only larger."

One of the most grotesque mythological animals of American origin comes from Illinois — a creation of the early Indians. On the Mississippi River between Alton and the mouth of the Illinois River is a sandstone cliff. About eighty feet above the river there were in the seventeenth century and until well into the nineteenth century two carved and painted representations of a monster known to the aborigines as the Piasa or "man-devouring bird." Father Marquette saw these figures in 1673 and described them as follows: "As we were descending the river we saw high rocks with hideous monsters painted upon them, and upon which the bravest Indian dare not look. . . . Each of these frightful figures had heads and horns like a goat; their eyes are red, beard like a tiger's, and face like a man's. Their tails are so long that they pass over their heads and between their legs under their bodies, ending like a fish's tail. They are painted red, green and black." Many legends prevailed among the Indians as to the ferocious nature of these monsters. The voice of one was said to be like the roaring of a buffalo bull; of the other like the scream of a panther. A full account of the Piasa birds is contained in the Illinois Historical Society *Transactions* for 1908.[26]

Of the many fabulous monsters reported by Vance Randolph from the Ozark region perhaps the most horrifying is the gowrow which terrorized rural Arkansas in the 1880's. As described in the legends, "The gowrow was a lizard-like animal about twenty feet long, with enormous tusks." Most of its time was spent in caves and under rock ledges. It was carnivorous and devoured numerous deer, calves, sheep, goats, and possibly humans.[27]

---

[26] Clara Kern Bayliss, "The Significance of the Piasa," *Transactions of the Illinois State Historical Society,* 1908 (Springfield, 1909), pp. 114-22.

[27] Randolph, *op. cit.*

WAMPUS CAT

The pride of Idaho is the wampus cat. According to Tryon, "its howl on a lonely night will curdle a crock of sourdough." A favorite pastime of the animal is snaring eagles. Nature has endowed the wampus cat with an amazing right forearm, which "works like a folding pruning hook on the pantographic principle."[28]

My concluding specimen is the snipe, *Scolopax Inexplicablis,* a bird widely used for initiating tenderfeet. It is said that snipe have been seen occasionally but never caught. As Tryon stated, "Legions of sharp-eyed young foresters, engineers, cruisers, cookees, rodmen, and hard-rock apprentices have made repeated, careful, and valiant attempts to corral one, but notwithstanding the bushels of careful advice and instruction handed out by the older hands in the party, success has not yet been attained. Seldom does the seasoned woodsman make the attempt; he is probably too discouraged to try again."[29]

The snipe is a kaleidoscope of colors and wears both fur and feathers. It possesses a small third auxiliary leg to the rear for take-off, landing, and balancing purposes, and its fiery eyes emit small showers of sparks. It is most unfortunate that such an interesting bird is so elusive.

These are a few examples of the scores of fantastic and outlandish animals, birds, reptiles, and fish with which the American imagination has filled the great outdoors.

To round out the subject of unnatural natural history, brief mention should be made of another category of animal lore, of somewhat more sophisticated character: the national vogue for shaggy-dog stories, starting in the 1920's. Two or three samples of this genre should suffice.

1. There is the tale of the horse who could pitch and field baseball superbly but who when asked by the team manager if he could bat replied, "Who ever heard of a horse that can bat?"

2. A man went to visit a friend and was amazed to find him playing chess with his dog. "I can hardly believe my eyes," he

---

[28] Tryon, *op. cit.*
[29] *Ibid.*

SNIPE

exclaimed. "That's the smartest dog I have ever seen." "Aw, he's not so smart," the friend replied. "I've beaten him three games out of five."

3. A horse walked up to a bar and asked for a martini with a dash of horse-radish. The bartender mixed it and handed it to him. The horse drank it and smacked his lips. "I suppose you think it is strange," said the horse, leaning over the bar, "that I should come in here and ask for a martini with horse-radish in it." "Hell, no," said the bartender. "I like it that way myself."[30]

Perhaps it would be proper to attempt to draw some philosophical conclusions on the basis of this discussion of apocryphal biology. Clearly most of this lore belongs in the realm of the tall tale. Such stories are usually handed down from one generation to another, polished and improved by time. The tales turn up in all regions of the country and have many points of similarity.

[30] Benjamin A. Botkin, "Shaggy dog" stories, in *Sidewalks of America* (Indianapolis, 1954), pp. 515-20. See also Eric Partridge, *The "Shaggy Dog" Story* (New York, 1954).

One authority has defined the tall tale as "an exuberant combination of fact with outrageous fiction." Frequently there is a tiny grain of truth somewhere in the most improbable yarn. In fact it has been suggested that improving on actual happenings rather than outright lying is the distinguishing feature of the tall tale. Nevertheless, the tall tale deals frankly with marvels, with the remarkable or prodigious.

As one of the foremost experts, J. Frank Dobie has pointed out, the genuine narrator of tall tales considers himself an artist. He knows what he is lying about and his listeners know also, unless they are greenhorns or tenderfeet, in which case, of course, they are fair game. Therefore, the narrator does not pretend to fool either himself or his audience. His object is amusement and recreation. Perhaps he needs no further excuse for existence.

ADDITIONAL REFERENCES

Bedichek, Roy, "Folklore in National History," in *Folk Travelers,* edited by Mody C. Boatright and others (Austin: Texas Folklore Society, 1953), pp. 18-39.

Davidson, Levette J., and Forrester Blake, editors, "Unnatural Natural History," in *Rocky Mountain Tales* (Norman: University of Oklahoma Press, 1947), pp. 257-92.

ACKNOWLEDGMENTS

The illustration of the Piasa Bird is from *Transactions of the Illinois State Historical Society* (1908, p. 117). Other illustrations in this chapter are from Henry H. Tryon, *Fearsome Critters* (Cornwall, N.Y., 1939), reprinted by permission of the author.

JOHN T. FLANAGAN

FOLKLORE IN AMERICAN LITERATURE

The twentieth century has seen many changes in the status of
man. Revolutionary innovations have occurred in transporta-
tion, in medicine, in warfare, in society, and in government.
And even the comparatively peaceful field of literary criticism
has not been immune to alteration. The traditional historical
or biographical criticism seems to have gone largely by the way-
side. Impressionism is likewise looked on suspiciously. Certainly
the typical critic is no longer a soul adventuring among master-
pieces and reporting his highly subjective reactions. Instead we
have critics concentrating on the exact meaning of a text and
often interpolating their own ideas between the lines. Or we
have critics piecing together the background of the author and
striving to trace his intellectual evolution. Or we have critics
levying on sociology and psychology and anthropology to support new readings. To me one of the most exciting and interesting approaches to literature in the twentieth century is provided by the study of folklore and its impact on writing.

Folklore is difficult to define, and I shall attempt no definition
here. In the broadest sense it includes arts and crafts and cus-
toms as well as the more obvious verbal forms. The artisan who
carved a figurehead for a clipper ship and the silversmith who

wrought old designs in metal were working as truly in the folk tradition as the ballad singer or the taleteller. The essence of folklore, after all, is *tradition,* and traditions are preserved in the popular mind naturally, unconsciously, and without recourse to documents or instruction. This concept, surely, is what the English antiquarian William J. Thoms had in mind in 1846 when he coined the word "folklore" to denote popular superstitions and popular antiquities. And this is what the folklorist understands today when he studies tales, songs, myths, legends, superstitions, riddles, and proverbs.

Very little of what is sometimes termed American folklore is actually native to North America. In pattern and style it is imitative of older forms, and most of it originated in the lands to the east of the Atlantic Ocean. But the miscellaneous peoples who make up the United States have not been derelict in preserving and amplifying the folklore which they or their ancestors brought with them to the New World. Nor have they on the whole failed to make fresh contributions. If few native American ballads have been found to equal the 305 English and Scottish ballads so diligently collected and studied by Francis J. Child (who was, be it noted, an American scholar), there are songs and tales which combine freshness with interest. Moreover, a land which has created or romanticized such stalwarts as John Henry, Johnny Appleseed, Davy Crockett, Mike Fink, Paul Bunyan, and Pecos Bill is certainly not lacking in genuine folk figures. And the easy accretion of myth and fantasy around historical names has already resulted in the magnification of Daniel Boone, Andrew Jackson, Buffalo Bill, and Abraham Lincoln into half-legendary heroes.

Folklore in American literature is almost as old as folklore in American life and certainly as constant. When Cotton Mather recorded how divine providence violently interfered with ordinary New England life, he thought he was writing ecclesiastical history but he was actually reporting folklore. Mather easily accepted specter ships, heavenly signs, the tormenting of innocent people by witches and devils; and he constantly gave allegorical interpretations to unusual phenomena. When Benjamin Franklin ironically remarked that the grand leap of the whale up the falls of Niagara was, to all those who had seen it, one of the most amazing events in nature, he was simply telling one of the best American tall tales. When Longfellow, a century later, confused a half-mythical Iroquois chieftain with an Algonquian trickster hero, he also interested a nation in Indian folklore, and he made the mythical courtship of Hiawatha and Minnehaha as much a national possession as the equally mythical rescue of Captain John Smith by Pocahontas. In our own day the poetry of Vachel Lindsay and Stephen Vincent Benét and the fiction of William Faulkner proves again the close relationship of folklore to literature. One of Faulkner's best stories, "The Bear," transcends a simple hunting tale by virtue of the mythical qualities attached to the bear itself and the contribution of the folk ritual to the gradual maturing of the story's protagonist, young Ike McCaslin.

For many decades critics, unaware of the enormous amount of folk material in American literature, ignored both the substance and the effect. Indeed it is only in the last twenty-five years that writers like Constance Rourke, Bernard De Voto, Richard Chase, Daniel Hoffman, and Arthur Palmer Hudson have affirmed in print the obligations of our authors to folklore. Today it is a commonplace to say that Mark Twain, Melville, Hawthorne, Irving, and Cooper, among the older figures, incorporated a good deal of folklore into their work, but the extent and importance of the material are even yet not generally understood. And we are seldom ready to admit that writers closer to us in time — Elizabeth Madox Roberts, Marjorie Kinnan Rawlings, Carl Carmer, John Steinbeck — are equally indebted. The average reader will concede the Uncle Remus stories to be plantation folklore and will grant that *Green Pastures* is based fundamentally on the simple anthropomorphism of Louisiana Negroes. But he forgets Eugene O'Neill's subtle use of voodooism and the theme of the

magical silver bullet in *The Emperor Jones,* and if he reads
Conrad Richter's trilogy of settlement in the early Ohio Valley
he is likely to be less impressed by the careful folk idiom than by
the picture of the pioneer woman and matriarch who dominates
the narrative.

The subject is of course a vast one, and as exciting as it is vast.
It would be possible to take almost every major American writer
from James Fenimore Cooper to Thomas Wolfe (admittedly one
might have a little trouble in this connection with Henry James)
and demonstrate, first, that each owed great obligations to folklore, and, second, that each used folklore to reinforce the artistic
impact of his work. But such a demonstration is not my present
purpose. Instead, I should like to concentrate on certain themes
and on certain authors.

Probably no legend is more persistent in American life than
that which relates to buried treasure. It makes no difference how
the original bullion or jewels were placed in the ground or by
whom: Captain Kidd, Jean Lafitte, or Jesse James. Gold lies
in the hills or under the waters, and tons of earth have been
displaced or scores of sunken vessels disturbed in the hope of
reclaiming it. Sometimes the Spanish conquistadores were the
original hoarders so that one has only to find the long-forgotten
cache or mine to become rich overnight, or at least to share his
wealth with the Bureau of Internal Revenue. The theme of
buried treasure runs sinuously throughout J. Frank Dobie's fascinating *Coronado's Children,* where mestizos dream of fabulous
wealth just around the corner. The hope of finding a fortune is
also the motivating force in one of the amusing episodes of John
Steinbeck's *Tortilla Flat.* In this tale of the California coast the
paisanos hunt in the woods on St. Andrew's Eve, convinced that
the hidden metal on this particular night will emit a pale phos-
phorescent glow. Eventually the treasure seekers think they see
such a pale glimmer and dig frantically, but all they can find is
a concrete elevation post placed there by the United States
Geodetic Survey. Probably the most memorable use of the

buried-treasure motif in American literature occurs in Edgar
Allan Poe's famous short story, "The Gold Bug." True to his
interest in cryptograms, Poe shifted the reader's attention from
the great wealth left by the pirates to the skill with which
Legrand unraveled the clues to its location. But nevertheless,
"The Gold Bug" deals with one of the favorite themes of folklore.

Ghosts or revenants are also fairly common in American
literature. Sometimes they are rather tangible figures, like Brom
Bones in Irving's "Legend of Sleepy Hollow," where the de-
tached head of the horseman proves to be a recognizable pump-
kin. Again they depend on the animation of the storyteller. The
Sam Lawson of Harriet Beecher Stowe's *Fireside Stories* is a
garrulous and shrewd rustic who entrances his domestic audience, but a modern reader finds his ghost lore less appealing
than his own exemplification of Yankee character. Somewhat
the same thing is true of Robert Frost's sparing use of the supernatural, although his poem "The Witch of Coös" is remarkably
atmospheric. Hawthorne's ghosts of the Boston Province House
tend to be skeletons exhumed from the library, garbed in the
interesting raiment of the historical novelist but important
chiefly as pegs on which to hang a moral. Certainly American
literature provides no counterpart for the spirit of Hamlet's
father or murdered Banquo.

But this is not to say that American authors have ignored the
spirits for whom the cockcrow is the daily knell. The local
colorists of the late nineteenth century created their share of
ghosts; one recalls the ha'nts who peopled the Tennessee mountain tales of Charles Egbert Craddock, and the wraiths who
flitted around corners in the French section of New Orleans so
well known to Cable and to Hearn. More recently Paul Green
of North Carolina has used with admirable effect the specters
who troubled the uneasy conscience of Negro murderers. In such
a short play as "In Aunt Mahaly's Cabin" he has provided a
truly grisly assemblage of demons and monsters: the Iron-Faced
Man, Jack-Muh-Lantern, Raw-Head-and-Bloody-Bones. More-

over, there has been a spate of stories about the vanishing hitch-
hiker, who usually turns out to have died sometime before he has
requested a ride. If the ghost seems in general not to have survived in the literature produced north of the Mason and Dixon
Line, it may be merely because clairvoyance flourishes best in a
milder climate.

Closely allied to ghost lore is witchcraft, and here New England comes into its own. Probably there is nothing more un-
savory in American history than the hysteria which engulfed
Salem in the 1690's and produced the infamous witchcraft trials.
It was to be expected that the subject would appeal to poet,
novelist, and dramatist. One of the best of the early American
plays, James Nelson Barker's *Superstition*, 1824, utilized witchcraft as a theme. Longfellow wrote an interesting closet drama
about the same subject, *Giles Corey of the Salem Farms.* The
accusation of sorcery produced the curse and the execution which
shape the plot of Hawthorne's *House of the Seven Gables,* and
the background of diabolical possession gives much of the dra-
matic effect to his fine short story, "Young Goodman Brown."
In our own day Esther Forbes has utilized similar material in her
carefully wrought novel *A Mirror for Witches,* and Arthur Miller
has written a telling drama entitled *The Crucible* which, although rather neglected in this country, found a warm reception
in Paris.

One might possibly argue that it is difficult in a modern age
to take either ghost lore or witchcraft seriously. It is perhaps
equally absurd to take phrenology or palmistry or telepathy seriously today, but all of these pseudo sciences had their following
in past decades. Moreover, they all represent the kind of trust
or conviction that defies scientific analysis and that remains long
after any logical basis for its existence has been shattered. But
traditions are rarely logical or realistic; they linger because they
are close to the heart of the people.

In general, superstitions remain current or assume different
forms, simple ones such as the belief that a criminal will return

to the scene of his crime, taboos against walking under a ladder and lighting three cigarettes from one match, conventions that require a successful fisherman to spit on his bait or a crapshooter to offer incantations over his dice. In *Tortilla Flat* John Steinbeck describes the afternoon sunshine on the water front at Monterey. The gentle wind ripples the bay and deepens the blue color. "Those lonely fishermen who believe that the fish bite at high tide left their rocks, and their places were taken by others, who were convinced that the fish bite at low tide." Superstition plays a considerable role in courtship though it is seldom so significant as Julia Peterkin makes it appear in her tales of Carolina plantation Negroes. In *Scarlet Sister Mary,* for example, the heroine is two-timed by her lover and in anger and dismay she goes to a conjurer in order to get a love potion. Neither petitioner nor magician doubts the efficacy of the charm. Another kind of superstition appears in Hawthorne's *House of the Seven Gables* where supernatural music is occasionally audible in that mansion of many angles and where flowers grow in a rare position high above the ground. All kinds of planting folklore and crop omens are employed by Elizabeth Madox Roberts in her sensitive novel of rural Kentucky, *The Time of Man.* Here ancient rituals and weather lore are far more important than the tested rules of scientific farming.

In that famous chapter of *Moby-Dick* called "The Whiteness of the Whale," Melville draws richly on folk connotation to establish his point that the color white is really ambivalent. White to an Occidental symbolizes virtue and sanctity; to an Oriental, mourning. White suggests cleanness and softness and spirituality; it may also connote sickness and decay and death. The albatross is a white bird and the white elephant of Siam is sacred. But leprosy is a white disease, Death rides on a white horse in apocalyptic time, and the albino to most people is repulsive. The whitened sepulcher is a familiar image, and the bleached bones of brutes and men terrify many a wayfarer. Yet a halo is often whitish, and the virgin adopts white as the symbol of purity. Some of Melville's illustrations are bookish and recondite; others depend more on the general experience of the reader for their effect. But it is quite obvious that the impact of the entire chapter depends on the folk associations of the examples.

A type of folk narrative especially prominent in American literature is the tall tale. A staple device in the oral humor of the old Southwest, it came into more permanent form through the writing of Thomas B. Thorpe, Augustus Baldwin Longstreet, George W. Harris, and Mark Twain. Thorpe's "The Big Bear of Arkansas" is one of the most anthologized of American short stories. To a half-amused, half-gullible audience in a cabin on a Mississippi steamboat a backwoods hunter boasts about the wonders of Arkansas, the creation state. He has once shot a wild turkey so fat that when the bird fell to the ground it burst and great gobs of tallow rolled out. He also remembers the sad case of the sow which lay down in a field where a few grains of corn had been scattered; during the night the corn germinated and grew so fast that the animal was killed by percussion. Indeed, as the hunter concludes wisely, Arkansas was intended for a hunting state; it is dangerous to plant things in its fertile ground. The climax of Thorpe's tale concerns the eventual death of an unhuntable bear, a beast which seemed impervious to knives or guns, which eluded pursuers by craft and strength, and which quietly succumbed when its time to die arrived.

It is perhaps needless to cite "The Celebrated Jumping Frog of Calaveras County," Mark Twain's classic story of the frog which lost a jumping contest because the owner of a rival frog filled its stomach with buckshot. But it should be noted that Twain not only told a superb anecdote but utilized a frame technique in the telling so that different styles of narration and idiom could be employed. Thus Simon Wheeler, the drawling narrator, is a character in his own right. William Faulkner told a singular tall tale in his early novel *Mosquitoes,* in which he described a worthy named Al Jackson who was a fishherder and who claimed ownership of most of the world's fish because he had notched their tails. Moreover, he began to raise sheep in the southern bayous but desisted when the sheep naturally took to their aquatic home and soon began to develop alligator scales. Tall-tale elements are, of course, familiar in the exploits of Paul Bunyan, Pecos Bill, and Febold Feboldson, all of whom perform incredible feats with a minimum of effort and generally defy the laws of nature. If Paul Bunyan can log off an upside-down mountain, Pecos Bill can ride the lightning. Moreover, Febold Feboldson's ranch was the scene of the original popcorn ball for the simple reason that he had planted a gigantic cornfield in a valley and some sugar cane on a hill. When the intense sunshine caused the corn to pop, the rain which followed washed the syrup out of the sugar cane and into the corn so that fusion was inevitable.

It might be well to add that even Melville's *Moby-Dick*, reduced to its simplest form, is nothing but a colossal tall tale. What else can be said of the mania of Captain Ahab which compels him to seek revenge on one specific whale and which persuades him that he can find this particular whale in a certain season of the year and in a definite part of the Pacific Ocean? I need not go into the explanations and details by which Melville succeeds in making the idea plausible. I speak here only of the tall-tale aspects of the novel.

Another interesting aspect of folklore is concerned chiefly with the verbal. I have reference to the folk speech, the slang, the wisecracks, the epigrams, the apothegms — in a phrase, the language of the folk. Benjamin Franklin was one of the first Americans to become proverb-conscious and to study and reshape maxims and adages. Some of the best of his sayings he put together into a remarkable sermon on prudence which is popularly known as "The Way to Wealth." Of course not all Franklin's wisdom relates to thrift, as one familiar proverb testifies: "Fish and visitors smell in three days." But he is best known for his defense of frugality and for the terseness and vigor of his advice.

In the nineteenth century a whole galaxy of American newspaper humorists and commentators employed the proverb or the wisecrack. Some of them, in addition, chose the illiterate pose and tried to reinforce their humor or wit by deliberate misspellings and faulty syntax. One remembers such figures as Josh Billings, Petroleum V. Nasby, and Lincoln's favorite, Artemus Ward. Of this group probably only Billings worked successfully within the framework of the proverb. Somewhat later Joel Chandler Harris incorporated plantation sayings into his Uncle Remus tales, and out in Kansas E. W. Howe proved his mastery of the trenchant paragraph. Examples must be used sparingly. But one cannot forget one or two of Harris' remarks: "Rooster makes mo' racket dan de hin w'at lay de aig," and "Watch out w'en you'er gettin all you want. Fattenin' hogs ain't in luck." As for Howe's acidulous comment, I shall always recall one observation probably because I share its prejudice: "Put cream and sugar on a fly, and it tastes very much like a black raspberry."

In our own day this combination of tartness, shrewdness, and folk idiom is evident in the sketches of Ring Lardner, in the platform wisdom of Will Rogers, and in the remarks of Abe Martin of Brown County, Indiana. The Hoosier sage was caustic about both social and political behavior. "If at first you do succeed," he once advised, "don't take any more chances." And about electioneering he observed: "You'd think some o' th' candidates wuz after th' woodpecker vote by th' way they tack ther cards on th' telephone poles." But no book has so captured the flavor and variety of popular speech as *The People, Yes,* by Carl Sandburg. Here, indeed, is the language of the folk, salty, banal, naive, cynical, language venturing from the anecdote to the apologue but always reflecting the lively, vigorous mind of the people. Like Franklin's proverbs, Sandburg's *The People, Yes* is a miscellany, a symposium, but it is placed within a matrix provided by the poet and it is fortunately impregnated with the poet's optimism. Where Franklin was often bitter or tart, Sandburg is assured and sanguine. Distrust leaders and policies as he may, in the people — the folk — he can always have faith.

Perhaps the best way to show the variety and value of folklore in American literature is to concentrate on the practice of certain authors. I have selected three examples of books which are steeped in folklore and where the folklore is organic rather than merely decorative. In these books the folklore is not only atmospheric and tonal; it even has structural importance. My examples are Mark Twain's *Huckleberry Finn,* George Washington Cable's *The Grandissimes,* and William Faulkner's *The Hamlet.*

Twain's debt to folklore has long been known but even today the extent of that debt is not generally recognized. As a boy in the hamlet of Florida, Missouri, as a youth in Hannibal, on the river and in the mining camps, Twain absorbed folklore as he absorbed life. Visits to the plantation of his uncle John Quarles gave him much of his material for later fiction, and friendship with the Negro hands enabled him to write so perceptively later of Nigger Jim. Both Huck and Jim are superstitious, credulous, aware of charms and omens. Both are rich in weather lore and quick to employ magic to avert ill luck. Jim believes implicitly in the virtues of a hair-ball, he uses string to tie up his kinky nigger wool into little tufts to fend off witches, he is rich in country lore. In conversation with Huck he alludes to the old belief that in the event of death one must inform the bees so that they will not become drones or vanish. Huck comments: "Jim said bees wouldn't sting idiots; but I didn't believe that, because I had tried them lots of times myself, and they wouldn't sting me."

Actually much of the behavior of the fugitive pair on the raft is motivated by their acceptance of popular superstition. Jim interprets weather signs and looks upon male hairiness as a sure sign of future wealth. Huck is convinced that his handling of a snakeskin is the reason for the catastrophe which results when a steamboat smashes into the raft. Moreover, when Huck is hiding out he knows that the citizens of St. Petersburg are searching for his supposed corpse in the usual ways since he hears the firing of a cannon and he sees a loaf of bread laden with quicksilver drifting down the current. In Twain's novel, folklore sets the tone of the early narrative, it reveals the mental processes of the chief characters, it often colors individual deeds, and it occasionally foreshadows later plot action. *Huckleberry Finn* is saturated with folklore, and it is a most convincing picture of early Middle Western life because of this very saturation.

My second example, Cable's *The Grandissimes,* is, as Edmund Wilson has recently stated, a much-neglected book. Cable was the best of the local colorists and a man who brought to his studies of Louisiana Creole life the knowledge and sensitivity of long intimacy with his subject. Three racial groups throng his stories: the Creoles themselves, descendants of the original French or Spanish settlers; Negroes or quadroons; and American interlopers from the North. The interrelationships of these groups and the contrasts between Yankee business efficiency and the indolence and fierce pride of the Creoles comprise Cable's fiction. *The Grandissimes* deals with the fortunes of a long-established and powerful Louisiana family which has become involved in various real-estate, commercial, and agricultural interests. But at the time of the cession of the territory to the United States in 1803 things are in a flux, and many of the old land grants seem suddenly invalid. The Grandissime family is hostile to the incoming Americans and is also determined to preserve the old hierarchy of the races. Desegregation is unheard of; even legal equality of white and black is absurd. Against a background of violence, duels, family feuds, Cable tells his story. The Creole is presented as sensitive, voluble, charming, and superstitious; the quadroon as friendly, loyal on the surface but fundamentally resentful, and more than willing to resort to voodooism when other means are denied him.

Madame Aurore Nancanou, the heroine, will not move into new quarters at 19 rue Bienville until she has carried into the empty house a new broom, a looking glass, and a silver coin. Moreover, she will admit no callers of a Monday, which is notoriously an unlucky day to receive guests, unless the front walk or banquette has been smeared with red paint. But she is not averse to having her quadroon servitor and friend work a spell so that Monsieur Agoussou, the voodoo demon of love, will be placated. And she would willingly pour a mixture of beer and sweet molasses on the front doorsill to propitiate Papa Lébat, the guardian of the doors through which suitors enter, if she could do so and escape detection.

When the quadroon Palmyre wishes to gain revenge on her master, she resorts to voodooism. She sees to it that a fresh egg, not cracked but smashed, is put outside the door of her victim, and she causes to be dropped in his path a small cloth bag containing dog and cat hair mixed with salt and pepper. Later Palmyre sends an acorn drilled with two small holes in which are inserted feathers, a section of a cornstalk filled with parings from a horse's knee bone, and a bunch of parti-colored plumes. These items, suggesting vividly the witches' caldron on the heath in *Macbeth*, excite the victim mildly. But when he finds on his doorstep "a small black-coffined doll, with pins run through the heart, a burned-out candle at the head and another at the feet," he turns cold with horror.

To the American doctor and the German pharmacist in the story, such actions seem pagan and senseless, but to the Creoles and quadroons the witchcraft is real and terrible. Superstition is close to their hearts, and the voodooism which was once practiced around Congo Square in old New Orleans is not to be trifled with. The theme of *The Grandissimes,* the family torn by feud and exacerbated by the breaking down of racial barriers, is generally above the level of folklore, but folklore motivates action in a way which nothing else could.

My third example, William Faulkner's *The Hamlet,* is almost without parallel in modern American fiction in its wealth of folk humor. For here are mingled in one volume most of the folklore motifs of which I have been previously speaking: the tall tale, the search for buried treasure, rural superstitions, proverbs, even the supernatural with a comic twist. In addition, Faulkner has filled the novel with details of back-country life which make it an interesting increment to the famous Yoknapatawpha County series. Fundamentally *The Hamlet* concerns the rise of Faulkner's most unscrupulous character, Flem Snopes, a redneck from the pine woods whose aim seems to be to rise as fast as opportunity presents and then to look, like the traditional boll weevil, for a home for his relatives. Flem is shrewd and calculating, neither loquacious nor demonstrative, quite immune to such feelings as generosity or fairness, self-centered and determined. He is a hard bargainer whether his object is a horse or a wife. Conflict in the novel is provided by the itinerant gossip and sewing-machine salesman, Ratliff. But Ratliff, although he is smart and likable, is eventually no match for Flem Snopes and goes down to defeat like the rest of the rustics. Yet it is Ratliff who tells some of the anecdotes and who envisages the wonderful scene in which Flem invades Hell itself and the Devil finds he has no soul to torture.

Cruel folk humor is apparent in several parts of *The Hamlet*. There is the early scene in which a horse trader gets rid of a worthless steed by changing the animal's color and by making him appear sleek and healthy through the device of inserting a valve beneath the skin and inflating the hide with a bicycle pump. This is paralleled by the later episode of the spotted ponies, in which wild and ornery beasts from Texas are auctioned off in a ramshackle corral. When the purchasers attempt to claim their animals, pandemonium sets in, they stampede through the gate, and the countryside is alive the next few days with fantastic stories of galloping hoofs and equine demons.

Country beliefs about sex and birth are intertwined with the narrative. The speech of one character, the schoolmaster I. O. Snopes, is replete with proverbs, giving him a specious reputation for wisdom. The exploits of Flem Snopes take on the character of folk heroism, and even his victims find occasional satisfaction in the old maxim that it is better to be shaved with a sharp razor than with a dull one. Probably the climactic event of the story as a folk tale is the ruse by which Flem Snopes unloads the Old Frenchman Place on Ratliff by burying coins and leading Ratliff to assume that a quantity of gold is secreted on the premises. For once Ratliff's cupidity is superior to his common sense.

These three novels, then, suggest the possibilities of the artistic use of folklore in serious fiction. In every case the folklore is organic and fundamental. The social level of the characters and the nature of their environment are such that folklore is natural and appropriate. Without the folklore elements the three novels would not only be weaker; they would be inconceivable.

It is needless, then, to labor the point. Almost from the time that American literature began, folklore has been an essential part of that literature, and has made it more authentic, more colorful, more artistic. The use of folklore varies, of course, with theme and author. But it has enriched poetry, drama, and especially fiction. Whenever a writer has wished to deal with the folk, he has been wise enough to introduce the lore of the folk. Without folklore the major works of Twain, Melville, Faulkner, Hawthorne would be poorer books, and if these names were removed from the scroll of our national achievement, our literature would suffer indeed.

REFERENCES

I. MAJOR WORKS CITED IN THE TEXT

Cable, George Washington, *The Grandissimes* (New York: Charles Scribner's Sons, 1912).

Clemens, Samuel L. (Mark Twain), *The Adventures of Huckleberry Finn* (New York and London: Harper & Brothers, 1912).

Connelly, Marc, *The Green Pastures* (New York: Farrar & Rinehart, 1929).

Dobie, J. Frank, *Coronado's Children* (New York: Literary Guild of America, 1931).

Faulkner, William, *The Hamlet* (New York: Random House, 1940).

———, *Mosquitoes* (New York: Liveright, 1927).

Forbes, Esther, *A Mirror for Witches* (Boston: Houghton Mifflin Company, 1954).

Green, Paul, *In the Valley and Other Carolina Plays* (New York: Samuel French, 1928).

Harris, Joel Chandler, *Uncle Remus, His Songs and His Sayings* (New York: D. Appleton & Company, 1909).

Hawthorne, Nathaniel, *The Complete Novels and Selected Tales of Nathaniel Hawthorne* (New York: Modern Library, 1937).

Howe, E. W., *Country Town Sayings* (Topeka: Crane & Company, 1911).

Melville, Herman, *Moby-Dick* (New York: Oxford University Press, 1947).

Miller, Arthur, *The Crucible* (New York: Viking Press, 1953).

O'Neill, Eugene, *Nine Plays* (New York: Modern Library, 1941).

Peterkin, Julia, *Scarlet Sister Mary* (Indianapolis: Bobbs-Merrill Company, 1928).

Richter, Conrad, *The Trees* (New York: Alfred A. Knopf, 1940).

———, *The Fields* (New York: Alfred A. Knopf, 1946).

———, *The Town* (New York: Alfred A. Knopf, 1950).

Roberts, Elizabeth Madox, *The Time of Man* (New York: Viking Press, 1926).

Sandburg, Carl, *The People, Yes* (New York: Harcourt, Brace & Company, 1936).

Steinbeck, John, *Tortilla Flat* (New York: Covici Friede, 1935).

Stowe, Harriet Beecher, *Sam Lawson's Oldtown Fireside Stories* (Boston and New York: Houghton Mifflin Company, 1899).

Thorpe, T. B., "The Big Bear of Arkansas," in *Tall Tales of the Southwest,* edited by Franklin J. Meine (New York: Alfred A. Knopf, 1930).

II. Criticism

Chase, Richard, *Herman Melville, A Critical Study* (New York: Macmillan Company, 1949).

De Voto, Bernard, *Mark Twain's America* (Chautauqua, N.Y.: Chautauqua Institution, 1933).

Flanagan, John T., "Folklore in the Novels of Conrad Richter," *Midwest Folklore*, II (Spring, 1952), 5-14.

Frantz, Ray W., Jr., "The Role of Folklore in *Huckleberry Finn,*" *American Literature*, XXVIII (Nov., 1956), 314-27.

Hoffman, Daniel G., "Irving's Use of American Folklore in 'The Legend of Sleepy Hollow,' " *Publications of the Modern Language Association of America*, LXVIII (June, 1953), 425-35.

————, *Paul Bunyan, Last of the Frontier Demigods* (Philadelphia: University of Pennsylvania Press, 1952).

Hudson, Arthur Palmer, *Folksongs of Mississippi and Their Background* (Chapel Hill: University of North Carolina Press, 1936).

Rourke, Constance, *American Humor* (New York: Harcourt, Brace & Company, 1931).